TOOLS IN THE TOOLBOX:
Life Lessons in God's Word

By: Deborah Harwood

Cover Art: Sally Bertine Greve

TOOLS IN THE TOOLBOX:
Life Lessons in God's Word

©2008 by Deborah Harwood

International Standard Book Number:
9780615265650

Cover Art: Sally Bertine Greve
Cover Image: Aevum Images

Unless otherwise noted, the Scripture quotations
are taken from
The Holy Bible, New International Version
©Zondervan

The Holy Bible, New King James Version
©Thomas Nelson Bibles

The Holy Bible, New Living Translation
© Tyndale House

Published by:
Life Lessons, LLC
dharwood@iinet.com

And we also thank God continually because, when you received the word of God, which you heard from us, you accepted it not as the word of men, but as it actually is, the word of God, which is at work in you who believe.

1 Thessalonians 2:13

Preface

Dear Reader,

The purpose for writing this book is to help you get closer to God and make the Bible (also referred to as the Word of God) real in your life. The Bible should not be treated as a history book, a nonfiction book, or a novel. The Word of God is the most important writing that God has ever given to us. The Word of God is His heart, His thoughts, His will, and His way. After all, God spoke the entire universe into existence through His Word.

Another purpose of this book is to help you appropriate (to make use of) the Word of God in your life. I have taken various Scriptures from the Bible and presented them in conjunction with a theme (life lessons, if you will). These life lessons are teachings by way of a witness, personal knowledge, or real life experiences with God and His Word. One of the keys to appropriating God's Word in your life is to confess it, to say it out loud until it becomes a reality deep down in your heart. When you confess the Word with your mouth, it settles into your heart and becomes a truth in your life. I have included confessions for just that reason.

Each lesson is concluded with a prayer. Instead of praying the problem, we should pray the promise. There are thousands of promises that are found in God's Word. These promises are just as true today as they were yesterday and will be forever. As you read God's Word, ask the Lord, with a sincere heart, to direct you to just the right Scripture for your situation or problem. The Lord is always faithful.

God is His Word. The Word of God is His love letter to you. God is talking to you, helping you, guiding you, and loving on you through His Word. If you were to meet a new friend, you would spend time talking to him or her in order to get to know the person. God is no different from your friend. The more time you spend with Him reading His Word, praying to Him, being quiet before Him, and meditating on His Word, the more you get to know Him. The great thing about God is that every word He speaks is forever true.

I pray that you will be blessed by reading *Tools in the Toolbox: Life Lessons in God's Word* and that it will help you grow increasingly closer to God!

Sincerely,

Deborah Harwood

IS THERE A GOD?

The Word of God:

In the beginning God created the heavens and the earth.

Genesis 1:1

By faith we understand that the universe was formed at God's command, so that what is seen was not made out of what was visible.

Hebrews 11:3

For you created my inmost being; you knit me together in my mother's womb. I praise you because I am fearfully and wonderfully made; your works are wonderful, I know that full well.

Psalm 139:13-14

Whoever does not love does not know God, because God is love.

1 John 4:8

Life Lesson:

Is there a God? The answer is either yes or no. If you answer yes, then you acknowledge that God exists and that every creation has a Creator. If you answer no, then you believe that creation came into being all by itself, by "nothing" exploding and creating something. Take a look at life around you. Reflect on the design of your body or the complexity of a nucleic acid that contains your genetic instruction (your DNA, for example). Examine how intricately each organ, each bone, and each cell work together to function in unison. Survey the world around you and all of the creatures here on earth. Observe the wonders of the high mountain peaks, the open ranges, the birds of the air, and the fish of the sea. Contemplate the universe. Our Earth is part of the Milky Way galaxy, which is *just one* of the more than 100 billion galaxies in the observable universe. This is creation. Everything that is created must have a creator. God is the Creator. God created the order, the design, and the vast complexity of the universe. God created you and me. God is love. He has created us to love and be loved by Him. Is there a God? This is a personal decision for each one of us. I encourage you to choose God, choose love

Confession:

God created the heavens and the earth. God fearfully and wonderfully made me. I choose You, God; I choose love.

Prayer:

Heavenly Father,

I am amazed by You. How awesome and beautiful are the works of Your hands. I thank You, Lord, the Creator of heaven and earth, for creating my inmost being and knitting me together. I stand in gratitude for all that You have done for me and for showering me with Your love. Amen.

GOD IS ...

The Word of God:
Adonai (Aramaic) – Master or Lord
Elohim (Hebrew) – the eternal Creator
El 'Elyon (Hebrew) – the Lord Most High
El Shaddai (Hebrew) – the God who is sufficient for the needs of His people
El 'Olam (Hebrew) – the everlasting God
Jehovah (Hebrew) – I Am who I Am.
Jehovah-jireh (Hebrew) – the Lord our Provider
Jehovah-ropheka (Hebrew) – the Lord our Healer
Jehovah-shalom (Hebrew) – the Lord our Peace
Jehovah-rohi (Hebrew) – the Lord our Shepherd
Elohay Selichot (Hebrew) – God of forgiveness
Elohay Mishpat (Hebrew) – God of justice
Yesha (Hebrew) – Savior
Immanuel (Hebrew) – God is with us.
Father, Son, and Holy Spirit
Alpha and Omega

Life Lesson:
In order to describe who God is, it is important to understand what God calls Himself. The name of God is more than a title. His name helps us appreciate God's attributes, character, and relationship to us. For instance, the name Elohim tells us that He is the eternal Creator. The name Jehovah-jireh informs us that He is our Provider. Jehovah-ropheka reveals to us that God is our Healer. As we learn the different names of God, our understanding increases, our faith continues to build, and our capacity to praise and worship Him is expanded. As we call out His name, we affirm His deity, His authority, His holiness, and His power. God's name brings, joy, love, praise, and reverence into our hearts. Just as you call out to someone

using his or her name, when you call out His name, you are connected with Him. God has given us His Word to help us to understand who He is and how to relate to Him. God, the Creator of the universe, stands behind His every word. Start now by confessing the names of God, and let those confessions go deep down into your heart. Acknowledge that He is the "great I AM." How great is our God.

Confession:

God is the great I AM. He is the Alpha and the Omega. The Lord is my Shepherd and my everlasting God.

Prayer:

Heavenly Father,

Thank You for being who You are, the great I Am. Whatever I need, You are. Thank You, Lord. Amen.

JESUS IS . . .

The Word of God:
In the beginning was the Word, and the Word was with God and the Word was God. He was with God in the beginning. Through him all things were made; without him nothing was made that has been made. The Word became flesh and made his dwelling among us. We have seen his glory, the glory of the One and Only, who came from the Father, full of grace and truth.

John 1:1-4, 14

For God so loved the world that he gave his one and only Son, that whoever believes in him shall not perish but have eternal life. For God did not send his Son into the world to condemn the world, but to save the world through him. Whoever believes in him is not condemned, but whoever does not believe stands condemned already because he has not believed in the name of God's one and only Son.

John 3:16-18

I am the Alpha and the Omega, the First and the Last, the Beginning and the End.

Revelation 22:13

Life Lesson:
Historically speaking, few would deny that Jesus walked this earth about 2,000 years ago, that He performed remarkable miracles, and that He died a horrible death on a Roman cross. Some call Jesus a prophet; others see Him as a great teacher; a few refer to Him as a great man. Jesus and all who follow Him know and call Him the Son of God. Jesus is God. The Word of God tells us that Jesus is the Word, became flesh, and dwelt us. If you are looking for truth in your life,

Jesus is the truth. He came from the Father, full of grace and truth. Jesus is the fulfillment of each one of the more than 300 Messianic prophecies recorded in the Old Testament (as the Messiah for the Jewish people and the Savior for the entire world). When C.S. Lewis, a popular British theologian, was asked, "Is Jesus God?" he responded:

I am trying here to prevent anyone saying the really foolish thing that people often say about Him: 'I'm ready to accept Jesus as a great moral teacher, but I don't accept His claim to be God.' That is the one thing we must not say. A man who was merely a man and said the sort of things Jesus said would not be a great moral teacher. He would either be a lunatic—on the level with the man who says he is a poached egg—or else he would be the Devil of Hell. You must make your choice. Either this man was, and is, the Son of God: or else a madman or something worse. You can shut Him up for a fool, you can spit at Him and kill Him as a demon; or you can fall at His feet and call Him Lord and God. But let us not come with any patronising nonsense about His being a great human teacher. He has not left that open to us. He did not intend to.

C.S. Lewis, *Mere Christianity*,
The MacMillan Company, 1960, pp. 40-41.

Confession:
Jesus is the Alpha and the Omega, the First and the Last, the Beginning and the End. Jesus is God.

Prayer:
Heavenly Father,
Jesus is the Alpha and the Omega. Help us to know Jesus and walk in His ways all of our days. Amen.

THE HOLY SPIRIT IS . . .

The Word of God:

Now the earth was formless and empty, darkness was over the surface of the deep, and the Spirit of God was hovering over the waters.

Genesis 1:2

Therefore go and make disciples of all nations, baptizing them in the name of the Father and of the Son and of the Holy Spirit.

Matthew 28:19

The wind blows wherever it pleases. You hear its sound, but you cannot tell where it comes from or where it is going. So it is with everyone born of the Spirit.

John 3:8

But the Counselor, the Holy Spirit, whom the Father will send in my name, will teach you all things and will remind you of everything I have said to you. Peace I leave with you; my peace I give you. I do not give to you as the world gives. Do not let your hearts be troubled and do not be afraid.

John 14:26-27

Life Lesson:

God the Father, God the Son (Jesus), and God the Holy Spirit. The three divine Persons of God unified in one. This is the Trinity. All three Persons of the Trinity, or God head, operate in unity and cannot be separated because each one is the whole of God. Water is a good example to help you understand the concept of the Trinity. The chemical composition of water is H_2O. Water can be liquid, steam, or ice. However, water is still composed of H_2O whether it is in the form of liquid, steam, or ice. God the Father, God the Son, and God the Holy Spirit are each the whole of God. God is in heaven, and His Son, Jesus, sits at His right hand. The Holy Spirit resides here on earth and in the children of God (those people have been born again). Once you are born again, you have the Holy Spirit of God living inside of you. The Holy Spirit of God will teach you all things. In John 14, the reference to the Holy Spirit in Greek is "paraclete," which means "one who consoles, one who intercedes on our behalf, a comforter or an advocate." The Holy Spirit is the Spirit of truth. You cannot touch the Holy Spirit, but like the wind, you can see the works of the Holy Spirit. The Holy Spirit only does those things that are the will of the Father. The Holy Spirit is alive and actively engaged in a beautiful ministry here on earth. He (the Holy Spirit) will guide you in the ways of the Lord. All you need to do is ask.

Confession:

I am born again, and the Holy Spirit lives inside of me. The Holy Spirit of God is my Counselor, and He will teach me all things.

Prayer:

Heavenly Father,

Thank You so very much for Your Holy Spirit living inside of me. I pray that I would always remain open to receiving all that Your Holy Spirit would teach me. Amen.

THE BIG PICTURE

The Word of God:

So God created man in his own image, in the image of God he created him; male and female he created them. God blessed them and said to them, "Be fruitful and increase in number; fill the earth and subdue it. Rule over the fish of the sea and the birds of the air and over every living creature that moves on the ground."

Genesis 1:27-28

The Lord God took the man and put him in the Garden of Eden to work it and take care of it. And the Lord God commanded the man, "You are free to eat from any tree in the garden; but you must not eat from the tree of the knowledge of good and evil, for when you eat of it you will surely die."

Genesis 2:16-17

The god of this world has blinded the minds of unbelievers, so that they cannot see the light of the gospel of the glory of Christ, who is the image of God.

2 Corinthians 4:4

Again, the devil took him to a very high mountain and showed him all the kingdoms of the world and their splendor. "All this I will give you," he said, "if you will bow down and worship me." Jesus said to him, "Away from me, Satan! For it is written: 'Worship the Lord your God, and serve him only.'"

Matthew 4:8-10

Life Lesson:
The age-old question is: "If there is a God, then why is there so much evil in the world?" The answer lies in God's Word. God tells us that He created the universe. God also created man in His own image. God's first words to Adam and Eve were words of blessing. They were told to increase in number, fill the earth, and subdue it. God gave them the "power of attorney" to rule over the earth, including the right to name every living creature (Genesis 2:19). Then God told Adam not to eat from the tree of the knowledge of good and evil. The serpent (Satan) came right away to challenge the Word of God (and continues to challenge God's Word to this day). Adam and Eve made the choice to disobey God and eat from the tree of the knowledge of good and evil. This caused the fall of mankind, and the whole world fell into sin. Therefore, Adam and Eve abdicated their power and gave Satan a "power of attorney" to rule the earth. That's right; God's Word tells us that Satan is the "god of this world." Further confirmation of this fact is found in the book of Matthew, where Satan tried to tempt Jesus. Satan told Jesus that he would give Jesus the "kingdoms of the world" if Jesus would bow down and worship him. (There would be no temptation if Satan did not have "rights" to the world.) Remember the job description for Satan is found in John 10:10: "steal, kill and destroy." When you observe stealing, killing, or destruction, you know this is from the "god of this world," Satan. This is not of God. God brings us "life and life abundant." God's first words out of His mouth were words of blessing to mankind. God loves us. God asks us to pray "Thy kingdom come, thy will be done on earth as it is in heaven." There is no stealing, killing, or destruction in heaven.

Confession/Prayer:
Our Father, who art in heaven, hallowed be Thy name, Thy kingdom come, Thy will be done on earth as it is in heaven. Amen.

MORE THAN JUST A PROMISE, IT'S ALIVE!

The Word of God:

For the word of God is living and active. Sharper than any double-edged sword, it penetrates even to dividing soul and spirit, joints and marrow; it judges the thoughts and attitudes of the heart.

Hebrews 4:12

I will bow down toward your holy temple and will praise your name for your love and your faithfulness, for you have exalted above all things your name and your word.

Psalm 138:2

This is the meaning of the parable: The seed is the word of God. Those along the path are the ones who hear, and then the devil comes and takes away the word from their hearts, so that they may not believe and be saved. Those on the rock are the ones who receive the word with joy when they hear it, but they have no root. They believe for a while, but in the time of testing they fall away. The seed that fell among thorns stands for those who hear, but as they go on their way they are choked by life's worries, riches and pleasures, and they do not mature. But the seed on good soil stands for those with a noble and good heart, who hear the word, retain it, and by persevering produce a crop.

Luke 8:11-15

Life Lesson:

God has exalted His name and His word above all things. If God exalts His name and His word above all things, then we as His children should follow His lead. The Word of

11

God is right and true and should be first place in your life. If God's Word says it, then we believe it. The Word of God is living and active, just like a seed. The Word of God is the seed, and your heart is the soil. Some can hear the Word, but Satan comes right away to steal the Word. If the Word is stolen, it cannot grow. Some have a heart like a rock; even though the Word is planted, it cannot take root. Others have heard the Word, but their hearts are filled with thorns (cares, riches, and pleasures of the world), which choke out the seed before it can grow. However, the heart with good soil produces a good crop. The Word of God is heard, planted, nurtured, and yields a good crop. The Word of God is God speaking to each and every heart. Your heart is attracted to those things that you most treasure. If you are focused on the cares of this world, then your heart is filled with thorns, and your crop will not be able to grow. If you really desire to fulfill God's divine plan for your life, then your attention is focused on the things of God's kingdom. Plant the seeds of the Word in your heart daily, believe in faith, take action in faith, and watch the seeds grow and bring forth "life and life abundant" for the kingdom of God.

Confession:

The Word of God is living, active, and alive in me. I have hidden Your Word, God, in my heart that I might not sin against You.

Prayer:

Heavenly Father,

Illuminate Your Word so that I can produce an awesome crop for Your kingdom. Amen.

ONE WAY

The Word of God:

Moreover, the Father judges no one, but has entrusted all judgment to the Son, that all may honor the Father.

John 5:22-23

I and the Father are one.

John 10:30

No one who denies the Son has the Father; whoever acknowledges the Son has the Father also.

1 John 2:23

Everyone who believes that Jesus is the Christ is born of God, and everyone who loves the Father loves His child as well.

1 John 5:1

Jesus answered, "I am the way and the truth and the life. No one comes to the Father except through Me."

John 14:6

Life Lesson:

Jesus is the way, the truth, and the life. No one comes to the Father (God) except through Jesus. There is only one way to the Father, and that is through Jesus. It is Jesus and Jesus only. Jesus is God. God is very clear in His Word that He does not want you to be worshiping any other gods. You might say, "Well, why does it have to be Jesus only? That seems very intolerant." My response to you is, "God has given us the framework for life, and He has told us that the only way to Him is through Jesus." He tells us what He expects from us, and He rewards those who choose to obey. We were made to worship Him. God is a jealous God and requires that we worship Him (Father, Son, and Holy Spirit) and Him alone. There is no room for other gods because God says, "You shall have no other gods before me." If you honor His commandments, He will show love to you for a thousand generations. He set forth His first commandment in Exodus 20:1-4:

And God spoke all these words: I am the Lord your God, who brought you out of Egypt, out of the land of slavery. You shall have no other gods before me. You shall not make for yourself an idol in the form of anything in heaven above or on the earth beneath or in the waters below. You shall not bow down to them or worship them; for I, the Lord your God, am a jealous God, punishing the children for the sin of the fathers to the third and fourth generation of those who hate me, but showing love to a thousand (generations) of those who love me and keep my commandments.

Confession/Prayer:
Heavenly Father,

Enlighten the eyes of my understanding, Lord. Show me the things in my life that are not of You and give me wisdom and strength to remove anything in my life that gets in the way of loving You. In Jesus' name. Amen.

DO YOU KNOW WHERE YOU WILL SPEND ETERNITY?

The Word of God:

How you are fallen from heaven, O Lucifer, son of the morning! How you are cut down to the ground, You who weakened the nations! For you have said in your heart: I will ascend into heaven, I will exalt my throne above the stars of God: I will sit also upon the mount of the congregation, on the farthest sides of the north: I will ascend above the heights of the clouds; I will be like the Most High. Yet you shall be brought down to Sheol, to the lowest depths of the Pit.

Isaiah 14:12-15 NKJV

Do not be afraid of those who kill the body but cannot kill the soul. Rather, be afraid of the One who can destroy both soul and body in hell.

Matthew 10:28

The Lord is not slow in keeping his promise, as some understand slowness. He is patient with you, not wanting anyone to perish, but everyone to come to repentance.

2 Peter 3:9

I am the Living One; I was dead, and behold I am alive for ever and ever! And I hold the keys of death and Hades.

Revelation 1:18

Life Lesson:

Do you know where you will spend eternity? You make the choice. You have a body, you have a soul (mind, will, and emotions), and you have a spirit. Your spirit will live on eternally. The question is whether your spirit will spend eternity in heaven or in hell. God tells us that He is "our Father who art in heaven" and that there is a heaven (it is mentioned throughout the Bible). He warns us about the place called hell. The Greek word for "hell" as used in Matthew 10:28 is *gehenna*, which is defined as "a place of torment or everlasting punishment." *God desires that no one should perish but that everyone should come to repentance and have eternal life in heaven.* However, He gave us the choice. We have to make that choice. We know from God's Word that Jesus came to this earth to pay the price for our sin. Jesus died on the cross and went down to hell to pay the price for our sin. Once that price was paid, He was raised from the dead and sits at the right hand of God the Father. God wants you to choose to make Jesus your Lord. Once you choose to make Jesus the Lord of your life, you are no longer under the dominion of Satan. When you make Jesus the Lord of your life, God will receive you as His child, and your eternal home is in heaven.

Confession/Prayer:

Heavenly Father,

I confess to You that I believe that Jesus is Lord and that He rose from the dead. Help me all of my days to walk in the ways of Jesus, my Lord and Savior. Thank You, Jesus, for eternal life in heaven. Amen.

TAKE THE CHALLENGE

The Word of God:

But I, when I am lifted up from the earth, will draw all men to myself.

John 12:32

Let us draw near to God with a sincere heart in full assurance of faith, having our hearts sprinkled to cleanse us from a guilty conscience and having our bodies washed with pure water.

Hebrews 10:22

Even the sparrow has found a home, and swallow a nest for herself, where she may have her young—a place near your altar, O Lord Almighty, my King and my God Blessed are those who dwell in your house; they are ever praising you.

Psalm 84:3-4

The Lord is near to all who call on him, to all who call on him in truth.

Psalm 145:18

For everyone who asks receives; he who seeks finds; and to him who knocks, the door will be opened.

Luke 11:10

Life Lesson:

There are many of you reading this book who are earnestly seeking God. You are seeking confirmation that Jesus is the Son of God. You have an open heart, you have sincerely studied various religions, and you have tried various avenues to get to the truth. I present to you today a challenge. I would ask you to read the Scriptures written above out loud slowly and then let them settle into your heart. I would encourage you to ask the Lord to "come near to you." Ask Him to "reveal in a very real and personal way that Jesus is the Son of God." Believe in your heart that God will reveal this truth to you. Jesus promises that He will draw all men unto Himself; take Him at His word. Call on Him in faith, and He will answer you. Knock, and the door will be opened; it is time to walk through.

Confession:

I am a seeker of You, Jesus. I am knocking on Your door, and it is opened to me.

Prayer:

Heavenly Father,

Even the sparrows find a place near You, near Your altar. Draw me close, dear Lord, I pray. Amen.

ARE YOU A CHILD OF GOD?

The Word of God:

Yet to all who received him, to those who believed in his name, he gave the right to become children of God— children born not of natural descent, nor of human decision or a husband's will, but born of God.

John 1:12-13

I am the way and the truth and the life. No one comes to the Father except through me.

John 14:6

That if you confess with your mouth, Jesus is Lord, and believe in your heart that God raised him from the dead, you will be saved. For it is with your heart that you believe and are justified, and it is with your mouth that you confess and are saved.

Romans 10:9-10

Everyone who calls on the name of the Lord will be saved.

Romans 10:13

I write these things to you who believe in the name of the Son of God so that you may know that you have eternal life.

1 John 5:13

Life Lesson:

God is love. God loves you and wants you to be His child. He wants you to be able to call Him Father. God tells us that no one can come to Him except through His Son, Jesus. Jesus is the only Way to God.

God has a gift of salvation for you, and He wants you to receive this beautiful gift. How do we receive this beautiful gift? We receive this gift of salvation by believing that Jesus is Lord and that He rose from the dead. How do you receive Jesus and believe in His name? You believe with your heart and confess with your mouth. Believing is not hoping for something in the future; believing is an assurance in your heart that what you believe is done right here and now. You are saved and become a child of God when you believe in your heart and confess with your mouth that Jesus is Lord and God raised Jesus from the dead. You have made your belief a reality with your faith and your confession. Remember that God is a "faith" God. He used his mouth and His faith to speak the world into existence. You are created in His image. You have become a child of God with your mouth, your heart, and your faith.

Confession:

I confess that Jesus is Lord and that Jesus was raised from the dead. I have been saved, and I am born again. I am a Christian. I am a child of God.

Prayer:

Heavenly Father,

I come to You in the name of Your precious Son, Jesus. I confess that Jesus is Lord, and I believe in my heart that You raised Jesus from the dead. I am now reborn. I am a Christian—a child of Yours. Thank You, Jesus. Amen.

BORN AGAIN?

The Word of God:

Consequently, just as the result of one trespass was condemnation for all men, so also the result of one act of righteousness was justification that brings life for all men. For just as through the disobedience of the one man the many were made sinners, so also through the obedience of the one man the many will be made righteous.

Romans 5:18-19

In reply Jesus declared, "I tell you the truth, no one can see the kingdom of God unless he is born again. Flesh gives birth to flesh, but the Spirit gives birth to spirit."

John 3:3, 6

I tell you the truth, no one can enter the kingdom of God unless he is born of water and of the Spirit. Flesh gives birth to flesh, but the Spirit gives birth to spirit.

John 3:5-6

Therefore, if anyone is in Christ, he is a new creation; the old has gone, the new has come!

2 Corinthians 5:17

Life Lesson:
Did you know that you are a spirit, you live in a body, and you have a soul? Man is a spirit because man is made in the image of God (Genesis 1:27), and "God is a Spirit" (John 4:24). When Adam and Eve chose to disobey the Lord and eat of the tree of the knowledge of good and evil, the fall of man occurred. This fall placed all of humanity in a state of sin because of Adam and Eve's disobedience to the Lord. We

do not have to live forever in a state of sin (darkness). The Word tells us that just as through the disobedience of one man (Adam) the many were made sinners, so also through the obedience of the one Man (Jesus) the many will be made righteous. When you confess Jesus as the Lord of your life and that Jesus was raised from the dead, your spirit inside of you has been reborn. *To be born again is a spiritual rebirth.* Your spirit is not just enhanced or built up; your old spirit of sin and the lordship of the devil are gone. You have a new spirit; the Holy Spirit of the Lord is now inside of you. You are officially a child of God. Remember that God loves everyone; however, you can only be called His child if you are born again. You are a new creation in Christ Jesus. The old has completely gone, and the fresh and new Spirit of God is inside of you! You are now a child of the King! You have been delivered from the darkness into the Kingdom of God.

Confession:

I am a new creation in Christ Jesus. The old has gone, and the new has come in my life, and I thank You, Jesus.

Prayer:

Heavenly Father,

Thank You that the old me is completely gone; I am a new creation in Jesus. I am Your child, and I have Your very Spirit inside of me. Amen.

YOU HAVE THE SPIRIT OF TRUTH

The Word of God:

But when he, the Spirit of truth, comes, he will guide you into all truth. He will not speak on his own; he will speak only what he hears, and he will tell you what is yet to come.

John 16:13

If the Lord delights in a man's way, he makes his steps firm.

Psalm 37:23

A man's steps are directed by the Lord. How then can anyone understand his own way?

Proverbs 20:24

Life Lesson:

So now that you are a Christian and have a brand new born again spirit, what is next? Your brand new spirit is God's Holy Spirit. God's Holy Spirit is called the "Spirit of Truth" and the "Counselor." The Holy Spirit will convict you of sin (what is wrong). He convicts, not condemns (for condemnation is from Satan). So as you encounter issues in your life, be assured that you have the Spirit of Truth living inside of you, guiding and leading you to make the right choices in your life. Don't let anyone tell you that God does not care about the small details in your life. Even the smallest of things are important to God. For instance, we had a large party last year for our lacrosse team. I had one Saturday to accomplish a list of activities two pages long. I was driving down the road, and the Holy Spirit impressed upon me to stop at the party rental place. (We needed ten tables and sixty chairs.) Now, party equipment does not seem like a big deal, certainly not something that would concern God. It was inconvenient for me to stop at the party rental store first, but I obeyed and stopped. As I was placing my order, the clerk remarked, "You ordered the very last of our party chairs two minutes before closing time!" I was pleased that I followed the leading of the Holy Spirit. My "every step" is truly directed by the Lord. The Lord really cares about all of the details of your life. Ask Him to help you, and keep yourself fine-tuned to the leading of the Holy Spirit. We serve an awesome God.

Confession:

The Holy Spirit of God lives inside of me and guides me in all truth. The Lord directs my every step.

Prayer:

Heavenly Father,

Thank You so very much for Your Holy Spirit, who lives inside of me. Whatever the problem, whatever the issue, and whatever the decision, the Holy Spirit will guide me in all truth. Lead on, Lord Jesus, lead on. Amen.

GOD IN YOU!

The Word of God:

Don't you know that you yourselves are God's temple and that God's Spirit lives in you? If anyone destroys God's temple, God will destroy him; for God's temple is sacred, and you are that temple.

1 Corinthians 3:16

Do you not know that your body is a temple of the Holy Spirit, who is in you, whom you have received from God? You are not your own; you were bought at a price. Therefore honor God with your body.

1 Corinthians 6:19

To them God has chosen to make known among the Gentiles the glorious riches of this mystery, which is Christ in you, the hope of glory.

Colossians 1:27

We are therefore Christ's ambassadors, as though God were making his appeal through us. We implore you on Christ's behalf: Be reconciled to God.

2 Corinthians 5:20

Life Lesson:

"You are that temple." God inside of you! Wow, that is powerful. So many of us think that God resides in a church building. The church building may be dedicated to God's use, but God does not take up residence inside the church building. Your body is the temple of God. Your body is God's house. The Holy Spirit came inside of you to take up residence the minute you were born again. As believers we must be continually conscious of this fact, listen to the inward leading of the Holy Spirit, and, most importantly, obey. You are called to honor God with your body. You are an ambassador for Jesus. That is right; you are an ambassador for the Lord Jesus. As an ambassador you are an official of the highest rank sent as an authorized messenger, or representative, of God. How you treat your body, the way you conduct your life, the words that you say, and the actions you take are important because you are an ambassador for Jesus. The world is looking to the body of Christ to find Jesus in them. God reaches out to the world around you through you. Christ in you, the hope of glory. What message are you sending today?

Confession:

My body is the temple of God's Holy Spirit. I choose to honor God with my body. Christ in me, the hope of glory.

Prayer:

Heavenly Father,

Thank You for Your Holy Spirit living inside of me. Help me to walk out my life as an ambassador for Jesus. Amen.

FAITH THE GOD PLEASER

The Word of God:

Without faith it is impossible to please God, because anyone who comes to him must believe that he exists and that he rewards those who earnestly seek him.

Hebrews 11:6

Now faith is being sure of what we hope for and certain of what we do not see.

Hebrews 11:1

So then faith comes by hearing, and hearing by the word of God.

Romans 10:17 NKJV

Life Lesson:

You cannot please God without faith. Real faith in God is based upon the Word of God. Faith is "being sure of what We hope for and certain of what we do not see." Moffatt's translation of this verse reads: "Now faith means that we are confident of what we hope for, convinced of what we do not see." Faith is not just hoping (sometime in the future, maybe); faith is believing (being sure of it right here and now). Hope looks to the future. Faith is here and now. There are two types of faith: natural faith, which believes with our senses (sight, touch), and a supernatural faith, which believes with our heart. In this life lesson, we are referring to a supernatural faith, which believes from the heart. Supernatural faith does not just agree with God's Word in your mind (mental assent), but really believes from your heart. How do we know whether you have heart faith or mind faith? When you are operating from your mind, you say, "Yes, I know that God's Word is true and that He will meet all my needs according to His glorious riches in Christ Jesus; however, I do not see that my needs are met." Heart faith says, "If God says that my needs are met, then they are met right here and now, even though I cannot see it." You do not keep your eyes on your facts and circumstances around you, but keep focused on His promise. *We are to walk by faith, not by sight.* Your faith connects you to God, and your faith pleases Him. God hears you confess and believe His Word (without fear or doubt); He will make good on it. When you operate in fear, doubt, and unbelief, you are taking sides against God's Word. Every person has been given a measure of faith. What you do with that faith is up to you. Hearing the Word of God strengthens your faith. Keep building your faith by daily reading, confessing, and believing the Word of God.

Confession:

I believe that God exists and that He rewards those who earnestly seek Him. I earnestly seek You, Lord, and I believe that Your Word is true in my life.

Prayer:

Heavenly Father,

Thank You so very much for Your Word. Help me make time for Your Word. I ask for revelation knowledge so that Your Word becomes real in my life. In Jesus' name I pray. Amen.

COVENANT AGREEMENT

The Word of God:

Then the word of the Lord came to him: "This man will not be your heir, but a son coming from your own body will be your heir." He took him outside and said, "Look up at the heavens and count the stars—if indeed you can count them." Then he said to him, "So shall your offspring be." Abram believed the Lord, and he credited it to him as righteousness.

Genesis 15:4-6

No longer shall your name be called Abram, but your name shall be Abraham; for I have made you a father of many nations. And I will establish My covenant between Me and you and your descendants after you in their generations, for an everlasting covenant, to be God to you and your descendants after you.

Genesis 17:5, 7 NKJV

And as they were eating, Jesus took bread, blessed and broke it and gave it to them and said, "Take, eat; this is My body." Then He took the cup, and when He had given thanks He gave it to them, and they all drank from it. And He said to them, "This is My blood of the new covenant, which is shed for many."

Mark 14: 22-24 NKJV

Then he said, "Here I am, I have come to do your will." He sets aside the first to establish the second. And by that will, we have been made holy through the sacrifice of the body of Jesus Christ once for all. Day after day every priest stands and performs his religious duties; again and again he offers the same sacrifices, which can never take away sins.

But when this priest had offered for all time one sacrifice for sins, he sat down at the right hand of God.

Hebrews 10:9-12

Life Lesson:

Did you know that our God is a covenant God? If you are born again, then you are under the New Covenant (absolute binding agreement) with God. The consideration for this covenant was bought with the blood of Jesus. God also made an everlasting covenant (old covenant) with Abram, whom God later called Abraham, which means "father of many nations." Abram acted in faith and believed God's Word that he would be a father of many nations even though he was a hundred years old and his wife was ninety years old. God and Abraham cut a blood covenant with each other using animal sacrifices (Genesis 15:9-10). Deuteronomy 28 sets forth the blessings in the old covenant and the curses for breaking the terms of the old covenant. The old covenant was the basis for the new covenant. The difference is that Jesus, who knew no sin, became sin for us and made the "once for all" sacrifice by dying on the cross for the whole world. Our sin is not covered; it has been completely taken away. Jesus has redeemed us from the curses of the law. We are not only forgiven when we confess our sins, but we are also cleansed from all unrighteousness. Jesus took your sin and gave you His robe of righteousness and right standing with God. We are under the new blood covenant. Praise the Lord!

Confession/Prayer:

My God is a covenant God. I am under the new blood covenant. Amen.

STOP, DROP AND PRAY

The Word of God:

God is our refuge and strength, an ever-present help in trouble. Therefore we will not fear, though the earth give way and the mountains fall into the heart of the sea, though its waters roar and foam and the mountains quake with their surging.

Psalm 46:1-3

Life Lesson:

The waters were roaring and foaming one day in July at summer church camp. My son and his middle school friends (twelve to thirteen years old) had just finished river rafting at camp and decided to take a swim. They jumped in with their shoes on because the bottom of the river was full of rocks. As they were swimming in the river, the boys heard Will yell for help. They turned just in time to see Will get sucked under the water by the current. Will was trapped and could not get up! The tongue of his shoe was stuck under a rock, and he was pulled under water. Immediately, the boys jumped out of the river. Before the boys at the camp went into action, they *stopped, dropped, prayed,* and asked the Lord for help. The boys jumped in the river right next to Will, but the mighty force of the river pulled them down past Will. They quickly got out and jumped in again. Again, they missed Will. The next time, they jumped "up river," and the current pulled them right to Will. The boys miraculously loosened Will from the rocks and pulled him to shore. Will was unconscious and not breathing. One of the boys on shore administered mouth-to-mouth resuscitation while another friend ran to get help. Will started breathing again. He was quickly taken to the nearest hospital, where the doctors examined him.

Will was fine. He was saved just in time. Will had a choice that evening to go home or to go back for the last night of summer camp. Will chose to go back to camp. This choice was such a blessing. The campers had not yet heard any news about Will, so the mood of the camp was quiet and solemn. When Will rode up to the camp, the young campers were surprised. They were so elated to see him! There was joy in the camp that evening. The next morning, the entire camp went down to the river. Will and others were baptized in the river that day. They were baptized in the very waters that tried to take Will's life. The Lord showed Himself strong and turned the *"life-taking"* waters into *"life-giving"* waters. Stop, drop, and pray. Whatever battle you are in, whatever struggles you are experiencing, call upon the Lord, and He will deliver you! The Lord is your strength and an ever-present help in the time of trouble—just ask Will.

Confession:

God is my refuge and strength and ever-present help in the time of trouble.

Prayer:

Heavenly Father,

You are always there to help us in the time of trouble. Remind me, Lord, to look to You first and always. Amen.

GOT WISDOM?

The Word of God:

The fear of the Lord is the beginning of knowledge, but fools despise wisdom and discipline.

Proverbs 1:7

Wisdom is supreme; therefore get wisdom. Though it cost all you have, get understanding.

Proverbs 4:7

The mouth of the righteous man utters wisdom, and his tongue speaks what is just.

Psalm 37:30

If any of you lacks wisdom, he should ask God, who gives generously to all without finding fault, and it will be given to him. But when he asks, he must believe and not doubt, because he who doubts is like a wave of the sea, blown and tossed by the wind. That man should not think he will receive anything from the Lord; he is a double-minded man, unstable in all he does.

James 1:5-8

Life Lesson:

In order to have a meaningful and godly life, we need the wisdom of God. The wisdom of God is supreme. How do you get wisdom? Diligently seek it. First, you must start with a fear (reverence, admiration, respect) of the Lord. Second, you must diligently seek the wisdom of God from Him and believe you are receiving it. *God tells us that He will give you His wisdom generously, if you ask.* Do not doubt, do not question, and do not second-guess. Open your heart and believe right as you're asking that the Lord is imparting unto you His wisdom. When you receive God's wisdom, be quick to obey and turn away from those activities that are not of God. The wise person learns from instruction and discipline. Before making key decisions in your life, before you start to pray, before taking action—ask God for His wisdom. Wisdom is supreme. Above all else, get wisdom!

Confession:

I diligently seek God's wisdom. God's wisdom is supreme in my life.

Prayer:

Heavenly Father,

You tell me that if I lack wisdom, I should ask, and You will give Your wisdom to me generously. I ask You today, Lord, impart unto me Your wisdom in every area of my life. I open my heart, spirit, soul, and mind to receive Your wisdom, Your understanding, Your knowledge. In Jesus' name. Amen.

HOW MUCH LOVE?
"PUTTIN' THE LOVE FROM ABOVE ON YOU"

The Word of God:

Whoever does not love does not know God, because God is love.

1 John 4:8

Love never fails.

1 Corinthians 13:8

The Lord your God is with you, he is mighty to save. He will take great delight in you, he will quiet you with his love, he will rejoice over you with singing.

Zephaniah 3:17

Life Lesson:

I was driving home with a car full of teenage boys. One of the great skills of a mother is to pretend you are invisible; in other words, just let the boys talk without interrupting. This particular day, these boys were saying, "Don't be hatin' on me," which is a teenager response when one of the other boys is giving him a hard time. Interpreted in plain language for the parents, this means, "Don't give me a bad time; be nice to me." As the conversation progressed, or should I say digressed, they started talking about another classmate in ways that were not positive. I decided that I needed to interject. "Have you tried puttin' the love on this classmate?" They looked at me funny because "puttin' the love" made no sense to them. "Have you tried puttin' the love from above on this classmate? You know, giving him a compliment, smiling at him, saying hi in the hallway, making conversation with him, asking him to sit at the lunch table you with—puttin' the love from above on him."

The love from above is the kind of love that we receive from God. The love that never fails! I told them, "The Lord delights in you boys, and He also delights in the classmate you were talking about. Mark my words, when you walk in God's love, your efforts will always succeed. So don't be hatin' on him; be puttin' the love from above on him." They smiled.

Confession:
God loves me. He takes great delight in me. He quiets me with His love. He rejoices over me with singing. Love never fails.

Prayer:
Heavenly Father,
When I think of Your love from above, I am filled with joy. I rejoice and am glad in my heart. Help me, Lord, every day to grow in Your love. Amen.

GUARD YOUR SENSE GATES
(GARBAGE IN/GARBAGE OUT)

The Word of God:

Above all else, guard your heart, for it is the wellspring of life.

Proverbs 4:23

Whoever believes in me, as the Scripture has said, streams of living water will flow from within him.

John 7:38

The good man brings good things out of the good stored up in his heart, and the evil man brings evil things out of the evil stored up in his heart. For out of the overflow of his heart his mouth speaks.

Luke 6:45

Life Lesson:

You make contact with the world through your senses: your eyes (sight), your ears (hearing), your mouth (taste), your nose (smell), and your body (touch)—collectively "your sense gates." Now that you have been reborn, you have the Spirit of God living inside of you, in your heart. The reference to "heart" in this Scripture is not your physical heart, but your reborn spirit, which is the Spirit of God. Just as your body needs to be fed daily with food for strength, your spirit needs to be fed daily with the Word of God for strength. Fill your heart with good from the Word of God so you can bring forth good in your life. Be mindful of what enters your "sense gates"— the books you read, the movies you watch, and the music you listen to, for they all go into the heart. We all have had that experience where we hear a "catchy tune," and then later on that day we are still singing that tune and cannot get it out of our head. However, if that "catchy tune" happens to be filled with bad words, we are feeding our heart (spirit) with garbage. Into your senses, into your head, and down into your heart. Your mouth will then find itself speaking good if you have filled your heart with good (God's Word), or evil if you have filled yourself with evil. Those who choose good from the Scriptures will find streams of living water overflowing from within them. So "above all else," guard your heart (whatever it takes), for out of your heart is the wellspring of life.

Confession:

No matter what it takes, I am going to guard my heart. I believe in You, Jesus, and streams of living waters flow from within me.

Prayer:

Heavenly Father,

I know that all things are possible with You, and I am asking You today to help me to make right choices in my life. I thank You, Father, for Your help. In Jesus' name I pray. Amen.

TAKE COVER!

The Word of God:

He who dwells in the shelter of the Most High will rest in the shadow of the Almighty.

I will say of the Lord, "He is my refuge and my fortress, my God, in whom I trust."

Surely he will save you from the fowler's snare and from the deadly pestilence.

He will cover you with his feathers, and under his wings you will find refuge; his faithfulness will be your shield and rampart.

You will not fear the terror of night, nor the arrow that flies by day, nor the pestilence that stalks in the darkness, nor the plague that destroys at midday.

A thousand may fall at your side, ten thousand at your right hand, but it will not come near you.

You will only observe with your eyes and see the punishment of the wicked.

If you make the Most High your dwelling—even the Lord, who is my refuge—then no harm will befall you, no disaster will come near your tent.

For he will command his angels concerning you to guard you in all your ways; they will lift you up in their hands, so that you will not strike your foot against a stone.

You will tread upon the lion and the cobra; you will trample the great lion and the serpent.

"Because he loves me," says the Lord, "I will rescue him; I will protect him, for he acknowledges my name.

He will call upon me, and I will answer him; I will be with him in trouble, I will deliver him and honor him.

With long life will I satisfy him and show him my salvation."

Psalm 91:1-16

Life Lesson:
Do you know that Psalm 91 is one of the best protection prayers in the Bible? There is a testimony from the 91st Infantry Brigade of the U.S. Expeditionary Army, which was preparing to enter combat in Europe during World War I. These soldiers were "green" (had never seen battle). Their commander (a devout Christian) gave each one of them a card, which contained Psalm 91. In faith, they recited Psalm 91 every day. These soldiers were engaged in the bloodiest of battles during World War I. *While other American soldiers who engaged in these battles had up to 90 percent casualties, the 91st Brigade did not suffer a single casualty!* So take cover! By faith, daily confess that the Lord is your Refuge, your Shelter, your God, in whom you trust. When I affirmatively "take cover" for the body of Christ, my country, and my family, I actually envision the Lord's wing of protection spreading out over us as I confess His promises and believe them to be true. God will rescue us and protect us, for we love Him and acknowledge His name.

Confession/Prayer:
Heavenly Father,
You are my Refuge, You are my Shelter, You are my God, in whom I place all of my trust. No harm can befall me, and no disaster will come near my home or my person. You command Your angels concerning me, and they guard me in all my ways; they lift me up in their hands so that I do not strike

my foot against a stone. I tread upon the lion and the cobra; I trample the great lion and the serpent. I acknowledge Your name, Lord, and You always answer me. You give me long life, and You show me Your salvation. Amen.

DO YOU BELIEVE?

The Word of God:

In that day, you will no longer ask me anything. I tell you the truth, my Father will give you whatever you ask in my name.

John 16:23

I tell you the truth, if anyone says to this mountain, "Go, throw yourself into the sea," and does not doubt in his heart but believes that what he says will happen, it will be done for him. Therefore I tell you, whatever you ask for in prayer, believe that you have received it, and it will be yours. And when you stand praying, if you hold anything against anyone, forgive him, so that your Father in heaven may forgive you your sins.

Mark 11:23-25

He replied, "Because you have so little faith. I tell you the truth, if you have faith as small as a mustard seed, you can say to this mountain, 'Move from here to there' and it will move. Nothing will be impossible for you."

Matthew 17:20-21

Life Lesson:
We are to pray to God; our Heavenly Father, in the name of Jesus, His Son. Whatever you ask in the name of Jesus (meaning in accordance with Jesus/the Word of God) our Father will give to you. Jesus teaches us to believe while you are praying that you have received your answer, even though it is not yet manifested in the natural. You are to believe God's Word because God said it, not because you can see or feel it. *Once you can see it or feel it, then it is not faith.* God said it, and it is true. Just as if I told my daughter that I purchased a new

dress for her; she would immediately believe that I purchased her a new dress, without having to see it. If you are a child of God, you have believed God's Word in faith for salvation. Therefore, you have faith. The key is to exercise your faith and hold fast to your faith. Do not undermine your faith with wrong confessions. Jesus said that all we need is faith as small as a "mustard seed." We must keep that mustard seed in the ground so it can grow and not dig it up with doubt, fear, and wrong confessions. Christianity is called the "great confession." You confess with your mouth and believe in your heart, and you are saved. You confess and turn from your sin, and your sins are forgiven and you are purified from all unrighteousness. You confess daily the promises of God's Word in faith, and the problems and issues in your life will be resolved. Start speaking to those mountains in your life. If you have a mountain of fear in your life, then speak to it: "The Lord has not given me a spirit of fear but of love and of power and of a sound mind." If you feel the pressures of the world, then confess: "No weapon formed against me shall prosper." These promises are from the Lord and are real today. Believe God's promises, confess them, hold fast to them, and watch your mountains disappear into the sea.

Confession/Prayer:

I do not doubt the Word of God. His promises are true in my life, and I believe them right here and now. My heart is open to receiving all that God has for me. I choose to walk in mountain-moving faith. Amen.

WANT TO KNOW THE FATHER? LOOK AT THE SON

The Word of God:

When he looks at me, he sees the one who sent me.

John 12:45

He is the image of the invisible God, the firstborn over all creation. For by him all things were created; things in heaven and on earth, visible and invisible, whether thrones or powers or rulers or authorities; all things were created by him and for him."

Colossians 1:15

I and the Father are one.

John 10:30

On that day you will realize that I am in my Father, and you are in me, and I am in you.

John 14:20

Jesus replied, "If anyone loves me he will obey my teaching."

John 14:23

Life Lesson:

If you want to know what God thinks, how He would react, and what He is like, then look to Jesus. Jesus and God are one. God is our Father, and He loves us as a Father. He wants us to learn how to walk in His ways, so He sent His Son to show us the walk, the "love walk." Jesus spent much of His time ministering to the needs of people one on one. He dared to speak with the tax collectors and prostitutes. He even touched the lepers (the untouchables) and ministered to the poor and oppressed. The works, words, and teachings of Jesus are found in the books of Matthew, Mark, Luke, and John (which are known as the Gospels). If you really want to get to know Jesus, spend time reading the Gospels. Be careful to pay special attention to all of the words written in red (which are the words spoken by Jesus). Note how He handled situations, how He goes directly to the heart of a given matter, how He took time away from the crowds to pray, and how He was never afraid to speak the truth. Above all else, Jesus continued to love people, even those who wanted to take His life. He moved with compassion. His heart was filled with love beyond description.

Confession:

Jesus, I am in You, and You are in me. I love You, Jesus.

Prayer:

Heavenly Father,

Fill my heart with Your love and compassion, I pray. Help me to obey. Show me the way. In Jesus' name I pray. Amen.

FAITH SHOES

The Word of God:

Do not be anxious about anything, but in everything, by prayer and petition, with thanksgiving, present your requests to God. And the peace of God, which transcends all understanding, will guard your hearts and your minds in Christ Jesus.

Philippians 4:6-7

For God has not given us a spirit of fear, but of power and of love and of a sound mind.

2 Timothy 1:7 NKJV

Life Lesson:
A high school with more than two thousand students can be overwhelming to a freshman boy, especially to a boy who came from a class of fifty students. Further, it is daunting to try out for a basketball team heavily populated with athletic superstars. My son came home and told me he was not trying out for basketball this year. I asked him, "Don't you enjoy basketball anymore, or are you afraid of not making the team?" He responded that there are some really good athletes at his new school, and he was afraid of not making the team. I replied, "If you are not trying out due to fear, then you have no choice but to try out. You cannot allow fear to operate in your life, for God has not given you a spirit of fear." My son went to bed that night and prayed, "Lord, I know that You know what I should do, so I have faith that You will work this situation out for me." As an act of faith, he went down to the shoe store three weeks before tryouts and bought a pair of basketball shoes (in his new high school colors). He and more than thirty other boys tried out for twelve open positions. The

last day of tryouts the coach announced that this year they decided to take fourteen players instead of twelve (a first in the history of this high school). My son was one of those players. God makes a way. God honors faith.

Confession:

I choose not to be fearful or anxious about anything. Whatever comes my way, I will present my requests by prayer and petition and with thanksgiving knowing that You, Lord, are more than enough. Your peace, which transcends all understanding, guards my heart and my mind in Christ Jesus.

Prayer:

Heavenly Father,

I am so thankful that You are my Father. Because You are my Father, there is nothing for me to fear. Thank You for watching over me. Amen.

THE POWER OF PRAISE

The Word of God:

This is what the Lord says to you: "Do not be afraid or discouraged because of this vast army. For the battle is not yours, but God's." Early in the morning they left for the Desert of Tekoa. As they set out, Jehoshaphat stood and said, "Listen to me, Judah and people of Jerusalem! Have faith in the Lord your God and you will be upheld; have faith in his prophets and you will be successful." After consulting the people, Jehoshaphat appointed men to sing to the Lord and to praise him for the splendor of his holiness as they went out at the head of the army, saying: "Give thanks to the Lord, for his love endures forever." As they began to sing and praise, the Lord set ambushes against the men of Ammon and Moab and Mount Seir who were invading Judah, and they were defeated.

2 Chronicles 20:15, 20-22

About midnight Paul and Silas were praying and singing hymns to God, and the other prisoners were listening to them. Suddenly there was such a violent earthquake that the foundations of the prison were shaken. At once all the prison doors flew open, and everybody's chains came loose.

Acts 16:22-26

Out of the mouth of babes and nursing infants You have ordained strength, because of Your enemies, that You may silence the enemy and the avenger.

Psalm 8:2 NKJV

48

Life Lesson:

Jehoshaphat sent his praise and worship team out front before the battle. Are you kidding? Jehoshaphat had been given a Word that the Lord would fight his battle. Jehoshaphat had faith and believed that the battle was the Lord's. As the Israelites began to sing and praise, the Ammonites, the Moabites, and the Meunites were completely defeated by the Lord. Praise brings the Lord into action, provides strength, and stills the enemy. Another wonderful example of the power of praise is found in the book of Acts. Paul and Silas were beaten, flogged, and put in the "inner prison." About midnight, they started singing hymns so loud that the other prisoners could hear them. The praise of Paul and Silas brought the Lord on the scene. The Lord caused an earthquake to occur. This earthquake caused the prison doors to fly wide open, and their chains were loosed. Yes, that's right, the very earth shook for Paul and Silas that night as they sang hymns of praise to the Lord. You are a child of the King, so next time in the battlefield of your life, the battlefield of your mind, call on Jesus and praise Him. Worship the Lord with all your heart and let Him show Himself strong on your behalf.

Confession:

I give thanks to You, Lord, for Your love endures forever.

Prayer:

Heavenly Father,

Let me continually offer to You a sacrifice of praise. I praise Your holy name. Amen.

HAVE YOU GIVEN FORGIVENESS?

The Word of God:

Therefore, I tell you, whatever you ask for in prayer, believe that you have received it and it will be yours. And when you stand praying, if you hold anything against anyone, forgive him, so that your Father in heaven may forgive you your sins.

Mark 11:24-25

Pray like this: Our Father in heaven, may your name be kept holy. May your Kingdom come soon. May your will be done on earth, as it is in heaven. Give us today the food we need, and forgive us our sins, as we have forgiven those who sin against us. And don't let us yield to temptation, but rescue us from the evil one. "If you forgive those who sin against you, your Heavenly Father will forgive you. But if you refuse to forgive others, your Father will not forgive your sins."

Matthew 6:9-15 NLT

Be imitators of God, therefore, as dearly loved children.

Ephesians 5:1

Life   Lesson:

If you are born again, you are a child of God and God is your Father. As children of God, we are to be imitators of our Father. We are to follow in His ways. If you want to receive from God, you will need to give forgiveness. He tells you that He will forgive you your sins as you have forgiven those who sin against you. Unforgiveness is a heart hardener, a blessing blocker, a device from the enemy! I remember one day while out for a walk, I started to pray for the President of the United States. During the prayer, I felt removed and very distant from God. I did not understand because I thought that the prayer for our President was important. Then the Holy Spirit brought to my attention (like a fish swimming by in a fish bowl) the name of a person I had known twelve years ago. The Holy Spirit reminded me that I had not forgiven that person. I immediately said to the Lord, "Oh, I am so sorry, Lord, for my unforgiveness. I forgive this person. Bless this person. Lord. Forgive me, Lord." Immediately after this prayer, I was back in touch with the Lord again and able to finish my prayers. You have to ask yourself this question: What is more important to you? Is it more important to you to hold that grudge, unforgiveness, anger, and hatred in your heart, or is your relationship with God more important? The choice is yours. Now, there are times where forgiveness comes more easily than others. In those instances when it is too hard to forgive the person on your own, go to the Lord and ask Him to help you forgive that person. In prayer, lift that person up to the Lord and place that person in the Lord's hands as you envision the Lord loving on that person. *Do not let anyone or anything come between you and your Father. Be quick to forgive.*

Confession/Prayer:
Heavenly Father,

The desire of my heart, Lord, is to be close to You. I do not want to let anything or anyone come between You and me. I forgive anyone who has ever sinned against me. With regard to those persons whom I have had a hard time forgiving, Lord, I need Your help so I can give forgiveness. I lift them up to You today and ask that You hold them, love on them, and heal our relationship, Lord. In the name of Jesus I pray. Amen.

SOUND MIND

The Word of God:

But we have the mind of Christ.

1 Corinthians 2:16

For God has not given us a spirit of fear, but of power and of love and of a sound mind.

2 Timothy 1:7 NKJV

Do not be anxious about anything, but in everything, by prayer and petition, with thanksgiving, present your requests to God. And the peace of God, which transcends all understanding, will guard your hearts and your minds in Christ Jesus.

Philippians 4:6-7

Life Lesson:

How many times have you heard people say when they forget something or misplaced something, "I think I am losing my mind," or, "Oh, I am getting so old, my memory is not very good"? If you are a born again believer, these types of confessions are not in line with what God has to say about you and your mind. God says you have the "mind of Christ." The mind of Christ means you know His redemptive plan, His will, and His purpose. The mind of Christ is the mind that is directed by the Spirit of God. God says you have a "sound mind." You are a member of the body of Christ. When you say you are losing your mind, you are making a confession contrary to the Word of God. You need to line up your confessions with the Word of God. Speak in faith and believe that what the Lord has to say about you is true. You have the "mind of Christ." We are to continually seek God and remain in His Word. If we choose to take everything to God in prayer and do not allow ourselves to be anxious about anything, then God's peace will come in and flood our hearts. The peace of God will guard both our hearts and our minds in Christ Jesus.

Confession:

I have the mind of Christ. I have a sound mind. The peace of God is guarding my mind in Christ Jesus.

Prayer:

Heavenly Father,

Thank You so very much for Your Word. I am a member of the body of Christ, and I have the mind of Christ. I ask You, Lord, to help me every day to stay in Your Word and to make Your Word my confession. Amen.

NOTHING MISSING, NOTHING BROKEN, WHOLENESS—SHALOM

The Word of God:

Peace I leave with you; my peace I give you. I do not give to you as the world gives. Do not let your hearts be troubled and do not be afraid.

John 14:27

Do not be anxious about anything, but in everything, by prayer and petition, with thanksgiving, present your requests to God. And the peace of God, which transcends all understanding, will guard your hearts and your minds in Christ Jesus.

Philippians 4:6-7

"Lord, if it's you," Peter replied, "tell me to come to you on the water." "Come," he said. Then Peter got down out of the boat, walked on the water and came toward Jesus. But when he saw the wind, he was afraid and, beginning to sink, cried out, "Lord, save me!" Immediately Jesus reached out his hand and caught him. "You of little faith," he said, "why did you doubt?"

Matthew 14:28-30

Life Lesson:

There are many references in God's Word to "God's peace." The peace of God is more than a calm feeling inside of you; it is so much deeper. Let's take a look at the Hebrew word for peace, which is "shalom." Shalom is defined as "peace, nothing missing, nothing broken, well-being and complete." When Jesus told you that He is leaving you with "His peace," that means He has blessed you with completeness in every area of your life.

Yes, you heard that right, completeness in every area of your life. Let that sink into your heart. Completeness (nothing missing, nothing broken) in every area of your life. How do we walk in that peace? By keeping focused on Jesus, by filling our thoughts with His love, by guarding our hearts, by meditating on God's Word, by walking in faith and not in fear, but trusting in God in every area of our lives. Just like Peter, who stepped out in faith and was able to walk on the water when his eyes were fixed on Jesus, this is the key to walking in peace. However, when Peter looked away from Jesus and focused on the waters around him, he became afraid and began to sink. The cares and worries of the world will bring you down, just like a boat anchor. Your hearts will become troubled and afraid, and you will sink in the waters of life, unless you firmly fix your eyes upon Jesus. Do not be anxious about anything, but take everything to God in prayer and believe that He will take care of it, and He will.

Confession:

I live in shalom. I am not anxious about anything, but in everything, by prayer and petition, with thanksgiving, I present my requests to God. The peace of God, which transcends all understanding, will guard my heart and my mind in Christ Jesus. Shalom.

Prayer:

Heavenly Father,

I am reminded of an old hymn. What a friend we have in Jesus, all our sins and grief to bear. What a privilege to carry everything to God in prayer. Oh what peace we often forfeit, O what needless pain we bear. All because we do not carry everything to God in prayer. Amen.

ACCESS GRANTED

The Word of God:

Then the man and his wife heard the sound of the Lord God as he was walking in the garden in the cool of the day, and they hid from the Lord God among the trees of the garden. But the Lord God called to the man, "Where are you?" He answered, "I heard you in the garden, and I was afraid because I was naked; so I hid."

Genesis 3:8-10

So the Lord God banished him from the Garden of Eden to work the ground from which he had been taken. After he drove the man out, he placed on the east side of the Garden of Eden cherubim and a flaming sword flashing back and forth to guard the way to the tree of life.

Genesis 3:23-24

Let us then approach the throne of grace with confidence, so that we may receive mercy and find grace to help us in our time of need.

Hebrews 4:16

In him and through faith in him we may approach God with freedom and confidence.

Ephesians 3:12

Life Lesson:

Before the fall of man, Adam and God spoke directly to each other. God walked in the Garden of Eden, and He and Adam spoke to each other. Adam had direct access to God right there in the Garden. Adam and Eve were made in the image of God and knew no sin, so they could be in the presence of God, until they sinned. All of mankind fell. They experienced fear for the first time, and they were driven from the Garden of Eden. Sin separated them from God. Sin cannot be in the presence of God. *ACCESS DENIED.* However, God never turned His back on mankind. He had a plan to redeem us. The plan was Jesus. Jesus was commissioned by God to accomplish redemption for us through His sacrifice made on the cross. Jesus is holy, and Jesus knew no sin. Jesus can be in the presence of God. Jesus is the "Way" back so that we may have direct access to God. In Jesus and through faith, we may approach God with freedom and confidence. *ACCESS GRANTED.*

Confession:
I am in Jesus, and He is in me. I approach the throne of grace with freedom and confidence.

Prayer:
Heavenly Father,
What an honor and what a privilege to be before Your throne of grace. I am so thankful that I have access to You. Thank You, Jesus! From a grateful heart. Amen.

HOUSE OF PRAYER

The Word of God:

After he had dismissed them, he went up on a mountainside by himself to pray.

Matthew 14:23

And as he taught them, he said, "Is it not written:
'My house will be called a house of prayer for all nations'?"

Mark 11:17

I want men everywhere to lift up holy hands in prayer, without anger or disputing.

1 Timothy 2:8

Devote yourselves to prayer, being watchful and thankful.

Colossians 4:2

Be joyful always; pray continually; give thanks in all circumstances, for this is God's will for you in Christ Jesus.

1 Thessalonians 5:16-18

The smoke of the incense, together with the prayers of the saints, went up before God from the angel's hand.

Revelation 8:4

Life Lesson:

You are a temple of the Holy Spirit. Are you making your temple a "house of prayer"? Prayer is essential to the life of any believer. We are to devote ourselves to prayer continually. We are to keep ourselves right before the Lord (without anger and disputing) and lift up our holy hands and pray. Jesus was fully devoted to prayer. There are many references to Jesus praying to God (His Father). We see Jesus praying over the children, praying for His disciples, praying for all believers, teaching the Lord's Prayer, going off by Himself to pray, praying before performing miracles, and proclaiming that the house of the Father will be a house of prayer for all nations. The Bible references the "prayers of the saints," which go up before God. The hand of the Lord moves with the prayers of His children. Your prayers are important. As a matter of fact, your prayers are critical to the accomplishment of God's kingdom work here on earth. Remember that you are a member of the body of Christ and Jesus is the Head of the body of Christ. Jesus has revealed to us "the way" we should walk here on earth. Jesus prayed! You should pray. If you have trouble knowing how to pray, ask the Holy Spirit to teach you. You can start by praying the Word of God. There are a number of prayers in the New Testament to pray: Matthew 6:9-13 (Lord's Prayer); John 17:20-25 (Jesus' prayer for all believers); Acts 4:23-30 (the believers' prayer); Ephesians 1:15-23 (thanksgiving and prayer); Ephesians 3:14-21 (prayer for Ephesians); Philippians 1:3-11 (thanksgiving and prayer); Colossians 1:3-14 (thanksgiving and prayer); 2 Thessalonians 1:3-12 (thanksgiving and prayer); and James 5:13-16 (prayer of faith).

Confession/Prayer:
Heavenly Father,

Teach me how to pray and give me strength to pray, as I should. My temple is a house of prayer. I devote myself to prayer, being watchful and thankful. Amen.

SWEET SLEEP

The Word of God:

When you lie down, you will not be afraid; when you lie down, your sleep will be sweet.

Proverbs 3:24

When you walk, they will guide you; when you sleep, they will watch over you; when you awake, they will speak to you.

Proverbs 6:22

I will lie down and sleep in peace, for you alone, O Lord, make me dwell in safety.

Psalm 4:8

Life Lesson:

Ever have trouble sleeping? Do you ever have nightmares that wake you up at night? So did my son, until he found Proverbs 3:24 one day and claimed it as his own. My son typed this verse and pinned it to his wall. Every night when he went to bed, he would recite this Scripture with me. I would say, "When you lie down," and he would respond, "I will not be afraid," and then I would say, "When you lie down," and he would respond, "my sleep will be sweet." This promise became real to my son. He confessed it every night. The last words he spoke before he went to bed were "my sleep will be sweet." Remember, these are not just any words; these are promises from God written in His Bible. God always honors His promises. These promises are activated in your life when you believe in your heart that they are true. Faith comes by

60

hearing and hearing by the Word of God. My son activated this promise of God through his faith and claimed it as his own. When he lies down, he always has "sweet sleep." You alone, O Lord, make me dwell in safety.

Confession:

When I lie down, I will not be afraid; when I lie down, my sleep will be sweet.

Prayer:

Heavenly Father,

I thank You for Your Word and Your promises. I know, Lord, that Your Word is true and You always honor Your Word. I pray that You open my heart to receive what You have for me and help me be obedient to Your Word. I know that when I lie down, I will not be afraid and that my sleep will be sweet because You said so. Thank You for my sweet sleep all of the days of my life. Amen.

THE HEART

The Word of God:

Jesus replied: "Love the Lord your God with all your heart and with all your soul and with all your mind."

Matthew 22:37

Fix these words of mine in your hearts and minds; tie them as symbols on your hands and bind them on your foreheads. Teach them to your children, talking about them when you sit at home and when you walk along the road, when you lie down and when you get up. Write them on the door frames of your houses and on your gates, so that your days and the days of your children may be many in the land that the Lord swore to give your forefathers, as many as the days that the heavens are above the earth.

Deuteronomy 11:18

The precepts of the Lord are right, giving joy to the heart. The commands of the Lord are radiant, giving light to the eyes.

Psalm 19:8

Above all else, guard your heart, for it is the wellspring of life.

Proverbs 4:23

And after the earthquake a fire, but the Lord was not in the fire; and after the fire a still small voice.

1 Kings 19:12 NKJV

Life Lesson

Did you know that the word "heart(s)" appears over 700 times in the Bible? Your heart is the wellspring of all of life. The Lord asks you to guard your heart. The Lord speaks right into our hearts, through the Holy Spirit, and tells us what is right and what is wrong. Every time you hear the voice of the Lord and you disobey, your heart hardens. The Word of God brings joy to your heart, gives light to your eyes and "life and life abundant" to you. We are also to teach our children the Word of God throughout the day. When your children wake up, when they lie down. When I used to drive my daughter and son to school, I would say as they started their day, "This is the day that the Lord has made," then they would respond in unison, "I will rejoice and be glad in it" (Psalm 118:24). Another tool I use to keep the Word alive is the posting of Psalm 103:1-5 by my bathroom mirror so I can see and confess it as I brush my teeth. When driving on the freeway and encountering rude drivers, I look at them as a prayer target. I choose to hold them up to the Lord and ask for the peace of God, which passes all understanding, to guard their hearts and minds in Christ Jesus. When I pass by an accident, I plead the blood of Jesus on the parties involved and ask that the Lord bless the hands of the emergency crew. When someone needs advice, I ask the Lord for wisdom (James 1:5) and ask that He provide me with a "word in season." Before going to bed, my children enjoy reading devotionals and ending each day in prayer. Make sure to keep the Word alive in your daily life. Whatever you do, keep the wellsprings of life flowing in your heart.

Confession/Prayer:

I purpose in my life to guard my heart, above all else, for it is the wellspring of life. I love the Lord my God with all my heart and with all my soul and with all my strength.

RELATIONSHIP/FELLOWSHIP

The Word of God:

You have made known to me the path of life; you will fill me with joy in your presence, with eternal pleasures at your right hand.

Psalm 16:11

On that day you will realize that I am in my Father, and you are in me, and I am in you. Whoever has my commands and obeys them, he is the one who loves me. He who loves me will be loved by my Father, and I too will love him and show myself to him.

John 14:20-21

Deep calls to deep, in the roar of your waterfalls; all your waves and breakers have swept over me.

Psalm 42:7

Life Lesson:

Relationship is the state of being related—kinship. Once you are born again, you are a child of God Most High. He is your Father, and you are His child. Okay, so now you have a relationship with God. Don't you want more than just to be related to God? Don't you want to fellowship with Him and find joy in His presence? This requires effort on your part. This requires time. Time spent worshiping the Lord. Time spent studying His Word. Time spent praying. Time spent alone with God. Time spent being quiet before Him. Time spent meditating (deeply pondering and reflecting) on His Word. Become aware of the leadings of the Holy Spirit and act on those leadings. Check your heart to determine if the Holy Spirit is telling you that your heart is filled with thanksgiving and gratitude, or if there is resentment and anger in your heart. The root of resentment is pride and self-pity, and its fruits are bitterness and envy. This is sin. God cannot fellowship with sin. We must be honest with God and be quick to confess our sin. As we turn from sin, we turn toward God, and we can have fellowship again. It is the desire of God's heart to spend time with you. He longs to be intimate with you. God wants more than a relationship with you; He wants a deep fellowship. Deep calls unto deep. It should be the desire of every believer's heart to know God and experience His close fellowship. To fellowship with God is the greatest of all privileges of God's children. Go ahead and dive in. Let God's waves and breakers sweep over you.

Confession:
You have made known to me the path of life. You, Lord, will fill me with joy in Your presence, with eternal pleasures at Your right hand.

Prayer:
Heavenly Father,
Forgive me, Lord, for being so complacent about my fellowship time with You. I desire to draw close to You. Touch me today, Lord; deep calls unto deep. Amen.

THE BLOOD OF JESUS:
THERE IS WONDERWORKING POWER

The Word of God:

Then Moses summoned all the elders of Israel and said to them, "Go at once and select the animals for your families and slaughter the Passover lamb. Take a bunch of hyssop, dip it into the blood in the basin and put some of the blood on the top and on both sides of the door frame. Not one of you shall go out the door of his house until morning. When the Lord goes through the land to strike down the Egyptians, he will see the blood on the top and sides of the door frame and will pass over that doorway, and he will not permit the destroyer to enter your houses and strike you down.

Exodus 12:21-23

How much more, then, will the blood of Christ, who through the eternal Spirit offered himself unblemished to God, cleanse our consciences from acts that lead to death, that we may serve the living God!

Hebrews 9:14

They overcame him by the blood of the Lamb and by the word of their testimony; they did not love their lives so much as to shrink from death.

Revelation 12:11

Life Lesson:
There is an old hymn called "There is Power in the Blood." The first few lines of that hymn are as follows:

Would you be free from the burden of sin?
There's power in the blood, power in the blood;
Would you o'er evil a victory win?
There's wonderful power in the blood.

There is power, power, wonder working power
In the blood of the Lamb;
There is power, power, wonder working power
In the precious blood of the Lamb.

The Lamb they are referring to is Jesus. In the Old Testament times, the Lord told the Israelites to put the blood of a lamb on the door frames of their homes so that the "destroyer" would not enter their homes and strike them down. We, too, are to acknowledge the power of the blood to defeat the devil, but it is not the blood of a real lamb. The power lies in the blood of Jesus, the Lamb of God (Jesus, who died for us and was resurrected). We do not place the blood of a real lamb on our door posts; rather, we speak or plead the blood of Jesus verbally in faith. We say to Satan, "Jesus conquered you at Calvary, and I plead the blood of Jesus on myself. You cannot touch me because I have the protection of the blood of Jesus." With our words, we daily "place," or plead, the blood of Jesus over our nation, our churches, our families, and our loved ones for protection. The Word of God tells us that we have overcome Satan by the blood of the Lamb and the word of our testimony. The blood of Jesus cleanses us from all sin, reconciles us to Christ Jesus, protects us from all evil, and makes us white as snow. There is power, power, wonder working power in the precious blood of the Lamb.

Confession/Prayer:
I plead the blood of Jesus on my nation, my church, my family, and myself. The blood of Jesus protects us. Amen.

WATCH YOUR WORDS!

The Word of God:

But I tell you that men will have to give account on the day of judgment for every careless word they have spoken. For by your words you will be acquitted, and by your words you will be condemned.

Matthew 12:36-37

Do not let any unwholesome talk come out of your mouths, but only what is helpful for building others up according to their needs, that it may benefit those who listen. And do not grieve the Holy Spirit of God, with whom you were sealed for the day of redemption. Get rid of all bitterness, rage and anger, brawling and slander, along with every form of malice. Be kind and compassionate to one another, forgiving each other, just as in Christ God forgave you.

Ephesians 4:29-32

When we put bits into the mouths of horses to make them obey us, we can turn the whole animal. Or take ships as an example. Although they are so large and are driven by strong winds, they are steered by a very small rudder wherever the pilot wants to go. Likewise the tongue is a small part of the body, but it makes great boasts. Consider what a great forest is set on fire by a small spark. The tongue also is a fire, a world of evil among the parts of the body. It corrupts the whole person, sets the whole course of his life on fire, and is itself set on fire by hell. With the tongue we praise our Lord and Father, and with it we curse men, who have been made in God's likeness. Out of the same mouth come praise and cursing. My brothers, this should not be.

James 3:3-6, 9-10

Life Lesson:

We have all heard the idiom, "Sticks and stones may break my bones, but words will never hurt me." This is not true! God's Word tells us, *"By your words you will be acquitted, and by your words you will be condemned."* "Do not let any unwholesome talk come out of your mouths, but only what is helpful for building others up according to their needs, that it may benefit those who listen." "Get rid of all bitterness, rage and anger, brawling and slander, along with every form of malice." Could it be clearer? Your words are critically important. The tongue corrupts the whole person when lips run wild with gossip, swear words, and evil reports. When you speak corrupt words, those corrupt words are like starting your life on fire; they send your life ship crashing and they cause your life to be out of control like a horse running wild. Our tongues are for praising the Lord, not for cursing man. Our tongues give us direction for our lives, just like a rudder on a ship points the ship in the direction it will travel. Whatever words you speak will turn your body, your life, and the way you will go. You have a choice—choose words of life and blessing!

Confession/Prayer:

Heavenly Father,

May the words of my mouth and the meditation of my heart be pleasing in Your sight, O Lord, my Rock and my Redeemer. Amen.

THE BLESSING

The Word of God:

God blessed them and said to them, "Be fruitful and increase in number; fill the earth and subdue it."

Genesis 1:28

I will make you into a great nation and I will bless you; I will make your name great, and you will be a blessing.

Genesis 12:2

The blessing of the Lord brings wealth, and he adds no trouble to it.

Proverbs 10:22

The Lord bless you and keep you; the Lord make his face shine upon you and be gracious to you; the Lord turn his face toward you and give you peace.

Numbers 6:22-24

Christ redeemed us from the curse of the law by becoming a curse for us, for it is written: "Cursed is everyone who is hung on a tree." He redeemed us in order that the blessing given to Abraham might come to the Gentiles through Christ Jesus, so that by faith we might receive the promise of the Spirit.

Galatians 3:13-14

Life Lesson:

The heart of the Lord is a heart to bless you. The first words out of the mouth of the Lord after He made Adam and Eve were words of blessing! Abraham was blessed by the Lord and was told that he would be made into a great nation.

He would be a blessing. The Lord instructed Moses how to bless the Israelites in the book of Numbers. The Lord is in the "blessing business." He tells us that His blessing brings wealth "with no trouble added to it." Christ has redeemed us, as born again believers, so that we might receive the blessings given to Abraham. How do we connect with the blessings that the Lord has for us? The answer is, through faith. We go to the Word of God, find those promises that relate to our situation. We then lay hold of those promises by believing what God has said and appropriate or speak those blessing promises over others and ourselves. The Lord wants us to act on His promises in faith, just like Abraham. Walk in the commandments of the Lord and start confessing those blessings listed in Deuteronomy 28:1-14. When you make the faith connection with the Lord, He pours out His blessings upon you.

Confession:

I am blessed in the city and blessed in the country. The Lord blesses me and keeps me, the Lord makes His face to shine upon me and is gracious to me, and the Lord turns His face towards me and grants me His peace.

Prayer:
Heavenly Father,

Thank You for being who You are, a God whose first thought toward mankind was to bless. Help me to walk in the blessing so I can be a blessing to all of those around me. Amen.

THE BLESSING BLOCKERS

The Word of God:

See, I am setting before you today a blessing and a curse—
the blessing if you obey the commands of the Lord your
God that I am giving you today; the curse if you disobey the
commands of the Lord your God and turn from the way that
I command you today by following other gods, which you have
not known.

Deuteronomy 11:26-28

Now it shall come to pass, if you diligently obey the
voice of the Lord your God, to observe carefully all His
commandments which I command you today, that the Lord
your God will set you high above all nations of the earth. And
all these blessings shall come upon you and overtake you,
because you obey the voice of the Lord your God: Blessed shall
you be when you come in, and blessed shall you be when you
go out.

Deuteronomy 28:1-2, 6 NKJV

"Teacher, which is the greatest commandment in the Law?"
Jesus replied: " 'Love the Lord your God with all your heart
and with all your soul and with all your mind.' This is the first
and greatest commandment. And the second is like it: 'Love
your neighbor as yourself.' All the Law and the Prophets hang
on these two commandments."

Matthew 22:36-40

Life Lesson:

I love to read Deuteronomy 28 because I love the
thought of all of God's blessings coming upon me and
"overtaking me." *Overtaken by blessings.* How does that happen?

72

Believe, love, and obey. Step number one: We need to believe that there is a God and love Him with all of our heart, soul, and mind. This means making Him the focus of our lives. We worship God in the way we live. We must remove everything in our life that would hinder or come in between God and us (confess our sin and turn away from it). We should read the Word of God and renew our minds daily. The second step is to love our neighbor as ourselves. This means love. "Love is patient, love is kind. It does not envy, it does not boast, it is not proud. It is not rude, it is not self-seeking, it is not easily angered, and it keeps no record of wrongs. Love does not delight in evil but rejoices with the truth. It always protects, always trusts, always hopes, and always perseveres. Love never fails." (1 Corinthians 13:4-8). Don't let your unforgiveness, impatience, envy, strife, and pride block your blessings. So God has given you a choice today. You can choose to walk in the blessings (see Deuteronomy 28:1-14) or curses (see Deuteronomy 28:15-68). It's your choice.

Confession/Prayer:
Lord, I make a choice today. I choose to walk in Your blessings. I choose to love You, Lord, with all my heart and with all my soul and with all my mind, and my neighbor as myself. I cannot do this without Your help, Lord. Help me walk the love walk. Amen.

"OUR FATHER WHO ART IN HEAVEN"

The Word of God:

For you did not receive a spirit that makes you a slave again to fear, but you received the Spirit of sonship. And by him we cry, "Abba, Father."

Romans 8:15

How great is the love the Father has lavished on us, that we should be called children of God! And that is what we are! The reason the world does not know us is that it did not know him.

1 John 3:1

And so we know and rely on the love God has for us. God is love. Whoever lives in love lives in God, and God in him.

1 John 4:16

Life Lesson:

If you are born again, God is your Father. He is not your mother, nor is He some nebulous being. God is your Father, your Dad, your Abba Daddy. He loves you with a love that cannot be described. God is love. He loves you so much that He gave His one and only begotten Son to die for you as a sacrifice for your sins. Many people have a hard time with "our Father" because they have not had a good father here on earth or they do not even know their father. This cause them to have a hard time relating to a Father who loves them. I have a young friend who told me she has no idea who her father is. As she was speaking, I could see her face wince with pain, and anger, and sadness all at the same time. I looked her straight in the eyes and said, "We have the same Father." Her eyes lit up as she looked at me, and then she tilted her head in a quizzical manner.

She asked, "We do?" I said, "Yes, we do. God is my Father, and He is your Father. He is the very best Father in the whole wide world." It was so beautiful to watch as a smile came to her face and her body was encompassed with peace. Don't let your earthly father relationship be a roadblock to your Heavenly Father relationship. Ask the Lord to help you get to know Him as your Father. He is always faithful. The desire of His heart is to grow close to you and to lavish His love on you with a love that cannot be described. The word "lavish" is defined as "with extravagance and profusion." That's exactly what happened to my little friend, the Lord lavished His love on her right before my very eyes!

Confession:

How great is the love the Father has lavished on me, that I should be called a child of God. And that is what I am, a child of God. God is my Abba Father.

Prayer:

Heavenly Father,

You are my Father, my Abba Daddy. Thank You, Jesus, for making the way back to the Father through Your sacrifice on the cross for my sins. What a perfect work, Jesus. What a perfect Father. Amen.

THE LOVE WALK

The Word of God:

"Teacher, which is the greatest commandment in the Law?" Jesus replied: " 'Love the Lord your God with all your heart and with all your soul and with all your mind.' This is the first and greatest commandment. And the second is like it: 'Love your neighbor as yourself.' All the Law and the Prophets hang on these two commandments."

Matthew 22:37-40

Life Lesson:

The greatest commandment is to love the Lord with all of our heart, with all of our soul, and with all of our mind. Are you doing it? Are you waking up in the morning and saying to the Lord, "I love You"? Is the Lord the affection of your heart? Do you long for His friendship? Do you obey His Word and the promptings of the Holy Spirit? Do you shrink back from public identification with Him? Do you open His Word with expectation and excitement? Do you love Him wholeheartedly? If not, then start today. God is waiting on you. Start when you wake up in the morning and lie down at night by confessing that you "love the Lord your God with all your heart and with all your soul and with all your mind." Ask the Lord to help you with your love walk. Turn to Him throughout your day and ask Him to show you the way. The second part of this love walk is "to love your neighbor as yourself." This love walk is unselfish and operates in forgiveness. It is a love that says, "I love you regardless of what you do." As we confess our love to God and our neighbors, we set our heart on God and what He would have us do. We start praying for the lost instead of our own needs. As we confess the Word of God concerning love, then His love will abound in our hearts and overflow to those around us. The love walk—start today.

Confession:

I love the Lord my God with all of my heart and with all of my soul and with all of my mind, and my neighbor as myself.

Prayer:

Heavenly Father,

Please forgive me for not loving You as I should. Help me to set my heart hard after You. Show me how to love You, Lord. I purpose to stir up the love that You have placed inside of me. Yes, Lord, they will know we are Christians by our love, by our love; yes, they will know we are Christians by our love. Amen.

PRAY THE PROMISE NOT THE PROBLEM

The Word of God:

My prayer is not for them alone. I pray also for those who will believe in me through their message, that all of them may be one, Father, just as you are in me and I am in you. May they also be in us so that the world may believe that you have sent me. I have given them the glory that you gave me, that they may be one as we are one: I in them and you in me. May they be brought to complete unity to let the world know that you sent me and have loved them even as you have loved me. Father, I want those you have given me to be with me where I am, and to see my glory, the glory you have given me because you loved me before the creation of the world. Righteous Father, though the world does not know you, I know you, and they know that you have sent me. I have made you known to them, and will continue to make you known in order that the love you have for me may be in them and that I myself may be in them.

John 17:20-26

Life Lessons:

Prior to the year 2001, most of my prayers were from memory or prayers focused on my problems. They were prayed from my mind and not from my heart. I knew I was missing something and started searching God's Word for answers. I noticed right away that Jesus always found time alone to pray. So if I am a follower of Jesus, then I should do as He did and find time to pray daily. Religions all over the world pray, but a Christian prays to God. I needed help focusing on God when I prayed, so I went to those places in my Bible that better reveal God (Ezekiel 1, 10; Isaiah 6; Daniel 7, 10-12; Revelation 19). Next I looked in God's Word for examples of prayers.

I found the prayers of Jesus (Matthew 6; John 17). I read the prayers in Psalms and the prayers for wisdom in Proverbs. I found the apostolic prayers (Ephesians 1, 3, 6; Philippians 1; Colossians 1, 4; 1 Thessalonians 2; 2 Thessalonians 3). These prayers are beautiful. I would encourage you to read them out loud. The reading of God's Word out loud helps you focus on the Word of God because the mind has a tendency to wander and stray from the Lord. As you are reading, your mind will quiet, and you will sense the presence of the Lord. When you do, pause gently and be quiet before Him. You are doing this to turn your mind and heart from the outward things of life to the inward deep parts of your being. In this place of quiet before the Lord, simply adore Him. Be sensitive to the leading of His Holy Spirit. During this time, He may have you take a Scripture and pray it, He may give you additional revelation knowledge regarding a Scripture, or He may have you just enjoy His presence. *He is waiting for you to seek Him. He is waiting for you to seek His Word and find the promise for the problem and then pray that promise in faith (believing when we pray that promise is true right now for our situation).* We have a loving Father who yearns to reveal Himself to you.

Confession/Prayer:
Heavenly Father,

I pray that all believers in Jesus may be one, Father, just as You are in Jesus and Jesus is in You. Amen.

ANGELS (PUT THEM TO WORK)

The Word of God:

Are not all angels ministering spirits sent to serve those who will inherit salvation?

Hebrews 1:14

Life Lesson:

I received a call from a good friend of mine. His mother (a Christian) had been ill, and she had to go to the hospital for an MRI. She did not want to have an MRI, so they gave her some drugs to calm her down. Her body did not react well to these drugs, and she became disoriented. She had a very serious drug reaction and did not want to be left alone. She was unable to be cared for at either the hospital or the assisted living home, so her son and daughter provided care in her home, twelve hours on and twelve hours off. My friend and I prayed together in agreement for his mother. During the prayer, the Lord revealed the following three Scriptures to us: (a) 2 Timothy 1:7 (KJV): "For God hath not given us the spirit of fear; but of power and of love and of a sound mind"; (b) 1 Corinthians 2:16: "But we have the mind of Christ"; and (c) Proverbs 3:24: "When you lie down, you will not be afraid; when you lie down, your sleep will be sweet." So we put these three Scriptures into action. We used our tools by appropriating the Word of God on behalf of his mother. We knew that every man has body, soul, and spirit. Just as you feed your physical body food, we set about feeding his mother's spirit spiritual food, the Word of God. Even though the drugs had affected his mother's mind, her spirit man remained awake and ready to receive. *The Word strengthens your spirit.* So my friend took the Word of God and read it to his mother. My friend is unusually talented and gifted with music, so he even put one of the verses to music and sang it to her. He knew that faith cometh by hearing and hearing by the Word of God. He sang the Word of God to his mother. Oh, what a beautiful song it was! Knowing that it was impossible to read the Word continuously, we charged angels on her behalf. Angels are ministering spirits, which can be directed by the body of Christ to minister the Word of God. So, in the name of Jesus, we commanded the angels to go to his mother and instructed them to continuously minister the three Scriptures mentioned above. Within a short period of time, his mother was able to sleep through the night. And to this very day, she is a new woman. Praise God for His Word in season, the keys that unlock the heart.

Confession:

God has given me angels as ministering spirits to serve me because I will inherit salvation.

Prayer:

Heavenly Father,

Thank You, Lord. Show us how to live out each day in Your ways. We thank You for our ministering spirits who are watching over us and helping us every day. Amen.

DO NOT LET THE SUN GO DOWN WHILE YOU ARE STILL ANGRY.

The Word of God:

Refrain from anger and turn from wrath; do not fret—it only leads to evil.

Psalm 37:8

A gentle answer turns away wrath, but a harsh word stirs up anger.

Proverbs 15:1

In your anger do not sin: Do not let the sun go down while you are still angry.

Ephesians 4:26

And hope does not disappoint us, because God has poured out his love into our hearts by the Holy Spirit, whom he has given us.

Romans 5:5

Life Lesson:

Satan will do whatever he can to put pressure on you, to shame you, to break you, to make you angry and walk in sin. Sin separates us from God. When you get angry, you say things that you do not mean. In anger, you confess fear, you confess hate, you confess unbelief, and you take actions that are not in love. Actions taken in anger are those that you will later regret. You have just given Satan exactly what he wants. You have given him access into your heart. Your sin ushers the devil right on into your heart and separates you from God. Whether you realize it or not, sin grants access to Satan, and unconfessed sin allows Satan to take up residence in your heart. Guaranteed, while Satan is in your heart, he will stir up all sorts of other trouble in your life because the Word says that Satan's job is to "steal, kill and destroy." The Word of God cautions us to guard our hearts above all else and fight anger with love. We are to respond with a gentle answer, which turns away anger. I know that this is easier said than done. One key that I have found is to keep my mouth closed and immediately say a prayer. On the spot, ask the Lord to help you. Walk away if you have to. We are to keep ourselves in check every day. We are to not continue to stew in our anger day after day. The Lord tells us that we are not to let the sun go down while we are still angry. Many people talk about anger management. We are not to manage anger; we are to get rid of it before the sun sets. Just like a sponge filled with water, when it is squeezed under pressure, out comes water. This is true with our hearts; God has poured out His love into your heart. Keep your heart full of His love so when you are under pressure and squeezed, out pours His love.

Confession:

I choose to walk in love. The love of the Lord is poured into my heart. My heart is filled to overflowing with the love of God.

Prayer:

Heavenly Father,

Thank You for pouring out Your love into my heart through Your Holy Spirit. Keep me in Your love every day. Amen.

BE TRANSFORMED

The Word of God:

Therefore, I urge you, brothers, in view of God's mercy, to offer your bodies as living sacrifices, holy and pleasing to God—this is your spiritual act of worship. Do not conform any longer to the pattern of this world, but be transformed by the renewing of your mind. Then you will be able to test and approve what God's will is—his good, pleasing and perfect will.

Romans 12:1-2

As water reflects a face, so a man's heart reflects the man.

Proverbs 27:19

Now the Lord is the Spirit, and where the Spirit of the Lord is, there is freedom. And we, who with unveiled faces all reflect the Lord's glory, are being transformed into his likeness with ever-increasing glory, which comes from the Lord, who is the Spirit.

2 Corinthians 3:17-19

Life Lesson:

"Offer your bodies as living sacrifices, holy and pleasing to God." There is such pressure in this world to conform to the ways of the world. We must not conform to this world, but allow the Holy Spirit to transform our lives. His Word renews our minds so that we can focus on Jesus. We are being transformed as we spend time with the Lord in prayer. We are being transformed as we spend time in worshiping the Lord. We are being transformed as we talk with the Lord and listen for His voice. We are being transformed into His likeness. *We are what we behold.* People who worship money become greedy. Those who worship themselves become arrogant. We worship God, and our faces reflect the face of His love. Just like a mirror. We reflect back His love. Every time you are in the manifest presence of the Lord, you are changed. God continues His beautiful work in each and every one of us, transforming us step by step into His likeness. As you allow the Word of God to get deep down into your heart, you receive revelation knowledge from the Holy Spirit. God speaks to us through His Word. Our minds are renewed every day as we spend time in His Word. We no longer conform to the ways of the world. We are being transformed into His likeness with ever-increasing glory, day-by-day and moment-by-moment.

Confession:

I reflect the Lord's glory and am being transformed into His likeness with ever-increasing glory.

Prayer:

Heavenly Father,

Thank You, Lord, for being Lord over my heart, my mind, and my life. Keep transforming me, I pray. Change my heart to your heart. In Jesus' name I pray. Amen.

USE YOUR ARMOR

The Word of God:

Be self-controlled and alert. Your enemy the devil prowls around like a roaring lion looking for someone to devour.

1 Peter 5:8

Therefore put on the full armor of God, so that when the day of evil comes, you may be able to stand your ground, and after you have done everything, to stand. Stand firm then, with the belt of truth buckled around your waist, with the breastplate of righteousness in place, and with your feet fitted with the readiness that comes from the gospel of peace. In addition to all this, take up the shield of faith, with which you can extinguish all the flaming arrows of the evil one. Take the helmet of salvation and the sword of the Spirit, which is the word of God. And pray in the Spirit on all occasions with all kinds of prayers and requests. With this in mind, be alert and always keep on praying for all the saints.

Ephesians 6:13-18

Life Lesson:

Be on the alert; the devil prowls like a roaring lion looking for someone to devour. Did you know that God has given you armor to protect yourself and stand against the devil? Just knowing about armor is not good enough. You need to suit up and use your armor. One day driving to school, my son felt his chest tightening. He said it was not serious. Together, we put on the full armor of God by speaking Ephesians 6 in faith. We thought that we had put on the full armor. We put on the belt of truth, the gospel of peace, and the helmet of salvation, held up his shield of faith, and took the sword of the Spirit. I dropped him off at school and went home to walk my dogs. As I was walking, the Lord impressed upon me that we had failed to put on the breastplate of righteousness. I sent him a text message reminding him to put on the "breastplate of righteousness." He obeyed, and there were no more chest pains. Hold up your shield of faith and tell Satan, "I am holding up my shield of faith in the name of Jesus, and every flaming arrow of yours is extinguished." Suit up and use your weapons.

Confession:

I am strong in the Lord and His mighty power. I put on the full armor of God, and I take my stand against the devil. I put on the belt of truth, the breastplate of righteousness, the helmet of salvation, the sword of the Spirit, the gospel of peace, and the shield of faith.

Prayer:

Heavenly Father,

What an honor it is, Lord, to be in Your army. Help me to remember to use my armor, Lord, and fight the good fight for Your kingdom. Amen.

HIS JOY/MY STRENGTH

The Word of God:

Do not grieve, for the joy of the Lord is your strength.

Nehemiah 8:10

But let all who take refuge in you be glad; let them ever sing for joy. Spread your protection over them, that those who love your name may rejoice in you.

Psalm 5:11

You have made known to me the path of life; you will fill me with joy in your presence, with eternal pleasures at your right hand.

Psalm 16:11

Shout for joy to the Lord, all the earth. Worship the Lord with gladness; come before him with joyful songs. Know that the Lord is God. It is he who made us, and we are his; we are his people, the sheep of his pasture. Enter his gates with thanksgiving and his courts with praise; give thanks to him and praise his name. For the Lord is good and his love endures forever; his faithfulness continues through all generations."

Psalm 100:1-5

Life Lesson:

Joy is more than being happy or pleased. Joy is the emotion of great delight caused by something exceptionally good or satisfying. Joy is elation. So when was the last time you were elated in your life? When was the last time you were delighted when you thought about God? When was the last time you made a joyful noise to the Lord? You can start today.

If you would like to be joyful, then start by entering His gates with thanksgiving and His courts with praise. Thanksgiving is lifting up your voice to God and thanking Him for all that He has done for you. You have just entered His gates. Then you start praising and worshiping Him. Worship is lifting up your voice to Him and praising Him for who He is. You are now entered into His courts. You are in His holy presence, His manifest presence. Every time you are in the manifest presence of the Lord, you are changed. You will discover a new strength in your life. You will find your thoughts directed to the Lord, His faithfulness in your life, and His magnificent love. Your praise can be soft, it can be loud, it can be spoken, or it can be sung. The Lord inhabits the praises of His people. Praise will lift you up and bring an encouragement to your spirit. You cannot dwell on the negative circumstances around you when you are singing praises. Affirmatively choose to start your day by coming to Him. "For the Lord is good and his love endures forever; His faithfulness continues through all generations."

Confession:

You, Lord, are my joy and my strength, my God, in whom I trust.

Prayer:

Heavenly Father,

I choose to start my day with praise. I worship you, Lord, with gladness and come before You with joy in my heart. Amen.

YOU ARE THE VICTOR, NOT THE VICTIM

The Word of God:

This is love for God: to obey his commands. And his commands are not burdensome, for everyone born of God overcomes the world. This is the victory that has overcome the world, even our faith. Who is it that overcomes the world? Only he who believes that Jesus is the Son of God.

1 John 5:4

And having disarmed the powers and authorities, he made a public spectacle of them, triumphing over them by the cross.

Colossians 2:15

No, in all these things we are more than conquerors through him who loved us.

Romans 8:37

What, then, shall we say in response to this? If God is for us, who can be against us?

Romans 8:31

We demolish arguments and every pretension that sets itself up against the knowledge of God, and we take captive every thought to make it obedient to Christ.

2 Corinthians 10:5

Life Lesson:

Each one of us has encountered various life difficulties. The enemy of our soul would love to have you dwell on each and every past negative situation in your life. He wants to play it over and over again. Satan would have you continue to focus on how you were wronged, who hurt you, and why life is not fair. You have to resist the devil. Take every thought captive and make it obedient to Christ Jesus. Remind yourself that you are in Jesus Christ and therefore you are more than a conqueror! You have overcome the world because you are in Jesus. You are alive in Christ. You have God on your side; who could possibly be against you? You are a world overcomer! That is right; you have the victory through Christ Jesus. "The victory over what?" you might ask. The victory over Satan and sin. Before you accepted Jesus as your Lord, you were dead to sin and under the dominion of the "god of this world." Now that you are in Christ, you are alive, and you have eternal life in heaven. Your sin has been bought and paid for by Jesus. This is not just the victory of going to heaven, but Jesus gave us the victory right now here on the earth. Take your place in Jesus Christ. You are a member of the body of Christ. The Head of the body of Christ is Jesus. Jesus is alive and is seated at the right hand of God the Father in heaven. Jesus is the victor, and so are you! Don't dwell on all of the past wrongs in your life. Let go of your self-righteousness and bitterness so that Jesus can bless you with His righteousness, love, and joy. Focus on Jesus and who He is. Start today and ask, "How can I be a blessing to others?" Walk in the victory.

Confession/Prayer:

Heavenly Father,

I am more than a conqueror in Christ Jesus. I have the victory in Christ Jesus. You are for me, God, so who can be against me? Amen.

GOD HONORS HIS WORD; HONOR YOURS

The Word of God:

God is not a man, that he should lie, nor a son of man, that he should change his mind. Does he speak and then not act? Does he promise and not fulfill?

Numbers 23:19

Do not lie to each other, since you have taken off your old self with its practices and have put on the new self, which is being renewed in knowledge in the image of its Creator.

Colossians 3:9-10

Be imitators of God, therefore, as dearly loved children.

Ephesians 5:1

Jesus Christ is the same yesterday and today and forever.

Hebrews 13:8

So shall My word be that goes forth from My mouth; It shall not return to Me void, but it shall accomplish what I please, and it shall prosper in the thing for which I sent it.

Isaiah 55:11

Life Lesson:

God does not lie. This statement sounds like something we should easily agree with. However, when we read His promises in the Bible, we disagree. We say to ourselves, "These promises were made yesterday and are not for today. We are quick to rely on our life experiences as opposed to God's promises. Some of us simply dismiss the Word of God as just some teaching stories or fables. No matter if it is Old Testament or New Testament, God is the same yesterday and today and forever, and His promises are true forever. As children of God, we are to take Him at His Word. God is looking for believers who will stand in faith on His Word. God's Word does not return to Him void. He says, "So shall My word be that goes forth from My mouth; It shall not return to Me void, but it shall accomplish what I please, and it shall prosper in the thing for which I sent it." (Isaiah 55:11) God is our Father, and we are His children. What He says is true. As His children, we are to imitate God. This means we are to stand in faith believing His promises in our lives. When we make promises to others, we are to honor those promises. God is our Father, and He honors His word. He expects us to do the same.

Confession/Prayer:

Heavenly Father,

Thank You for being who You are, a Father of truth who never changes. Help me to honor my word and be renewed in You daily. Amen.

STEAL, KILL AND DESTROY THE WORD

The Word of God:

The thief (Satan) comes only to steal and kill and destroy; I have come that they may have life, and have it to the full.

John 10:10

Now the serpent was more crafty than any of the wild animals the Lord God had made. He said to the woman, "Did God really say, 'You must not eat from any tree in the garden'?"

Genesis 3:1

In the beginning was the Word, and the Word was with God, and the Word was God.

John 1:1

Life Lesson:
The Word of God is God. So it should come as no surprise that Satan opposes God. When God created Adam and Eve, the first words out of Satan's mouth were words of challenge. Satan questioned Adam and Eve, "Did God really say . . .?" Nothing has changed with time. Satan's weapon is the power of suggestion. Satan is still battling God and challenging His Word. When you hear people say, "The Bible is too hard," or, "It takes too much time," or, "I am just so busy I cannot find time to read the Bible," guess who is still battling God's Word? Satan's job description is spelled out clearly in John 10:10: "steal and kill and destroy." You have the authority to resist Satan in the name of Jesus, and the Word says that Satan has to flee. Send him "packing" today so you are able to get into God's Word and grow in the Lord. In the morning, read some Scriptures and allow God to speak to you through

these Scriptures. You may read them out loud, slowly, or repeat them. Take time to pause and be silent after reading. The Word of God is God speaking to you. If the Holy Spirit moves you, read another Scripture. He may have you pray the previous Scripture. Speaking out in prayer is acting on God's Word. Speaking will cause you to believe in God's Word because it will settle into your heart. Do not let Satan distract you or encourage a wrong confession. Once God has revealed His Word for a certain situation in your life, stay with it until you see it manifested. In the beginning was the Word, and the Word was with God, and the Word was God.

Confession:

God, Your Word is You, and You are life and life abundant.

Prayer:

Heavenly Father,

I love Your life and life abundant. Help me to discern the ways of the evil one and set myself apart from him. I want only You, Lord, only You. Amen.

WHAT IS YOUR CONFESSION TO YOUR HIGH PRIEST?

The Word of God:

Therefore, since we have a great high priest who has gone through the heavens, Jesus the Son of God, let us hold firmly to the faith we profess.

Hebrews 4:14

Life Lesson:

Did you know that if you are born again, you have a High Priest? Yes, that is right. Jesus is your High Priest. Well, what does that mean to me? When we think of the term "high priest," most people think of a senior clergyman. In the Old Testament, the high priest was the person who represented the people before God and offered the various sacrifices prescribed by the law. Jesus was the Lamb of God and offered Himself as the complete "once and for all sacrifice" for the sins of all of mankind. He sits at the right hand of God and represents us before God. He acts on our behalf. That's right; Jesus is acting on your behalf before God Almighty. So Jesus is our High Priest. What are we confessing to the Lord when we approach Him? Are we crying out, "Oh, I am so tired; oh, I am so weak; oh, I do not know what to do; poor me." Well, that is not a confession that our High Priest can work with. These are not confessions written in His Word. God does not promise us a life of being tired and weak. It is time, then, to start your confession to your High Priest by confessing God's Word. The Word of God says, "The joy of the Lord is our strength." The Word of God says in Exodus 15:2, "The Lord is my strength and my song." The Word of God says in Psalm 18:32, "It is God who arms me with strength and makes my way perfect." Now you start confessing the Word of God in faith to your High Priest, and He can and will act on those confessions.

Your faith will build up inside of you as you continue to confess the Lord is your strength and your song. Before you know it, you will be feeling strong!

Confession:

Jesus is my High Priest. I am a child of the King.

Prayer:

Heavenly Father,

What an honor and what a privilege to come to You. Because of Your sacrifice, Jesus, we can come to the Lord directly. Jesus made the way. Jesus, you are the way maker. Forgive me, Lord, for all of my confessions over my life and the lives of others that are not in line with Your Word. Help me to confess Your Word, Your truth, and Your life. In Jesus' name. Amen.

MAKE YOUR MOVE

The Word of God:

What good is it, my brothers, if a man claims to have faith but has no deeds? Can such faith save him? Suppose a brother or sister is without clothes and daily food. If one of you says to him, "Go, I wish you well; keep warm and well fed," but does nothing about his physical needs, what good is it? In the same way, faith by itself, if it is not accompanied by action, is dead.

James 2:14-17

But everyone who hears these words of mine and does not put them into practice is like a foolish man who built his house upon the sand. The rain came down, the streams rose, and the winds blew and beat against that house, and it fell with a great crash.

Matthew 7:26-27

Life Lesson:

So we read the Word, we confess the Word, and we believe the Word. What more do we need to do? We have to put our faith into action. I had a "faith action" moment in my life, right after 9/11. My heart was stirred on behalf of all of the families who lost loved ones and for our country. I wanted to pray for them, but I did not know how to pray faith-filled prayers. I had a deep desire to know the Lord better and specifically asked Him to teach me how to pray. Day by day, He would work with me in His Word and teach me how to pray His Word. He also put the perfect teachers and teachings in my path. Then the Lord placed forming a prayer group on my heart. This was not something I wanted to do, and I did not feel qualified, so I did not take action. However, over the course of a couple of weeks, through conversations with various individuals, it was clear that the Lord was saying to me that I was to start a prayer group. I said to the Lord, "I cannot do this on my own. You will have to put this together and provide me with the teachings." So I stepped out in faith, and within forty-eight hours, each person the Lord spoke to me about was available. I made my move. God made His move. Just like a chess game, I moved in obedience, and He made His move. The prayer group is still meeting and going strong. The Lord is forever faithful as He continues to work with me every day to teach me how to pray.

Confession:

I am alive in Christ Jesus. I am a person of faith in God's Word. I am faithful to take action on what the Lord has placed on my heart to do.

Prayer:

Heavenly Father,

I am so very thankful for Your Word and the Holy Spirit. Your Word is a light unto my path and a lamp unto my feet. May I always hear only the voice of the good Shepherd (Jesus) and be quick to obey and take action. In Your precious name I pray, Jesus. Amen.

IT IS AGREED

The Word of God:

Again, I tell you that if two of you on earth agree about anything you ask for, it will be done for you by my Father in heaven. For where two or three come together in my name, there am I with them.

Matthew 18:19

How could one chase a thousand, and two put ten thousand to flight, unless their Rock has sold them and the Lord had surrendered them?

Deuteronomy 32:30 NKJV

Life Lesson:

If two of you agree about anything you ask, it will be done for you by the Lord. There is power in the "prayer of agreement." The key to this statement is praying the promise in unity with God's Word. This means at the time that you are praying with another believer, you both are in "one accord," or, to put it another way, you both "believe and stand on a promise of God together in agreement." If the children of God would only embrace this promise and make it real in their lives, then you would have every one of us every day finding a member of the body of Christ and praying the prayer of agreement in the hallways, on the street corners, or in the grocery stores. Individually, through the power of God's Holy Spirit and faith, we are mighty in prayer. However, when two or more of us come together in the prayer of agreement, our prayers are super charged. United prayers of agreement of two or more have a greater effect than the sum of the efforts of each individual. The Word says we can do ten times as much in prayer with the prayer of agreement than we can just praying by ourselves. So get into the Word and get into agreement.

Confession:

I know that when I and a Christian brother or sister agree about anything we ask for, it will be done by my Father in heaven. When two or three of us come together in the name of Jesus, there Jesus is with us.

Prayer:

Heavenly Father,

Thank You for Your Word and Your promises true. I love the prayer of agreement. Thank You, Jesus, for joining us whenever two or more come together in Your name. What an encouragement; what a promise; what love. Thank You, Lord. Amen.

FAVOR OF GOD

The Word of God:

For surely, O Lord, you bless the righteous; you surround them with your favor as with a shield.

Psalm 5:12

For the Lord God is a sun and shield; the Lord bestows favor and honor; no good thing does he withhold from those whose walk is blameless.

Psalm 84:11

May the favor of the Lord our God rest upon us; establish the work of our hands for us—yes, establish the work of our hands.

Psalm 90:17

A good man obtains favor from the Lord, but the Lord condemns a crafty man.

Proverbs 12:2

Life Lesson:

Are you feeling down? Is your mind filled with thoughts of worthlessness, shame, and embarrassment? Do you have low self-esteem? You need to realize right here and now that those thoughts of worthlessness are from Satan. You need to understand that you are a child of God and He surrounds you with His favor, just like a shield. You should say, "I have the favor of God! He loves me, and I love Him!" "God Almighty is my Father, and He blesses me with His favor!" The Word says that the Lord blesses the righteous, those who walk blameless and those who are good. Take a careful look at your life; how is your walk? Has the Lord been convicting (not condemning) you of certain things you need to change? Well, it is time. Time to correct them so you can walk in the favor of God. Continually seek the Lord for guidance, then take action and obey His Word. People who are disobedient do not walk in the favor of God. Stay with God, stay in His Word, obey Him, trust Him, and seek Him with all your heart. Believe for the increase of His favor. He will shower His wonderful blessings upon you! May the favor of God rest upon you and establish the work of your hands, now and forevermore.

Confession:

I have the favor of God! He loves me, and I love Him! God Almighty is my Father, and He blesses me with His favor!

Prayer:

Heavenly Father,

I love it, the favor of God. Thank You, Lord, for surrounding every part of my life with Your favor, just like a shield. Thank You for blessing me with Your favor so that I can be a blessing to others. Amen.

"BACK OFF"

The Word of God:

Submit yourselves, then, to God. Resist the devil, and he will flee from you.

James 4:7

The devil said to him, "If you are the Son of God, tell this stone to become bread." Jesus answered, "It is written: Man does not live on bread alone."

Luke 4:3-4

Be careful to follow every command I am giving you today, so that you may live and increase and may enter and possess the land that the Lord promised on oath to your forefathers. Remember how the Lord your God led you all the way in the desert these forty years, to humble you and to test you in order to know what was in your heart, whether or not you would keep his commands. He humbled you, causing you to hunger and then feeding you with manna, which neither you nor your fathers had known, to teach you that man does not live on bread alone but on every word that comes from the mouth of the Lord.

Deuteronomy 8:1-3

Life Lesson:

There are two forces in the world—good and evil—God and Satan. It is up to you to choose how you will walk. God is love, and He gives us His commandments to protect us. God wants you to have "life and life abundant." Life and life abundant comes directly from God and from obeying His Word. We are to live on every word that comes from the mouth of the Lord. On the other hand, Satan's job

104

description is to "steal, kill and destroy." When you have something in your life that is being destroyed, hurting you, stealing from you, condemning you, trying to bring you down, then you know that is Satan's handiwork. When evil strikes, do what the Lord tells you to do: Submit to Him and resist Satan. How do you submit to God? You come to Him, you listen to Him, and you obey His voice. How do you resist Satan? You do not follow his leadings, and you do exactly what Jesus did when Satan tried to tempt Jesus. Jesus did not put up His fists and try to physically fight. Jesus did not run and hide and feel sorry for Himself for being picked on. Jesus spoke in faith to Satan. He said, "It is written" and then quoted the Word of God in faith. Jesus wants you to do the same. You say, "Back off, Satan, in the name of Jesus; you cannot have me or my family. It is written, Resist the devil, and he will flee. You have to go now in the name of Jesus." And the Word of God promises Satan will flee. Nice!

Confession:

I submit myself and my life to God. I daily resist Satan, and he shall flee.

Prayer:

Heavenly Father,

I submit myself and my life to You today, Lord. All that I am and all that I have is Yours, Lord. Remind me to use Your Word as a help in my life and to tell Satan, "It is written, I resist you; you have to flee." Amen.

THE NAME ABOVE ALL NAMES

The Word of God:

Therefore God exalted him to the highest place and gave him the name that is above every name, that at the name of Jesus every knee should bow, in heaven and on earth and under the earth, and every tongue confess that Jesus Christ is Lord, to the glory of God the Father.

Philippians 2:9-11

For the husband is the head of the wife as Christ is the head of the church, his body, of which he is the Savior.

Ephesians 5:23

Life Lesson:

Earlier on in this book we addressed the different names of God. This verse in the Bible tells us that the name of Jesus is "above every name." Not only is the name of Jesus above every name, but at the name of Jesus "every knee should bow." So if there was any doubt in your mind what God thinks about Jesus, this verse should make it crystal clear to you. You cannot get any higher than the name above every name and at His name every knee should bow. So, you might ask, "How does that relate to me?" As a member of the body of Christ, you have legal standing to use the name of Jesus. A power of attorney, if you will. The name of Jesus carries with it all power in heaven, on earth, and under the earth. God said, "that at the name of Jesus every knee should bow, in heaven and on earth and under the earth." For instance, if you see a police officer out directing traffic, you know that individually, he does not have the power to stop the cars. But when he holds his hand out for the cars to stop, they do so because the police officer has the authority and backing of the entire police department.

When you invoke the name of Jesus (in faith of who He is and what that name means), it is not by your authority, but by and through Jesus. You have all of heaven backing you because God said so. When you have faith and believe on the name of Jesus, you are united with Him. You are empowered as a member of the body of Christ to go out and do God's kingdom work in the name of Jesus.

Confession:

I am a member of the body of Christ. At the name of Jesus, every knee should bow, in heaven and on earth and under the earth.

Prayer:

Heavenly Father,

Thank You for Your Son, Jesus. I pray, Father, that You help me embrace the name of Jesus and use His name as I should. Amen.

RESOLVE IT

The Word of God:

If your brother sins against you, go and show him his fault, just between the two of you. If he listens to you, you have won your brother over. But if he will not listen, take one or two others along, so that 'every matter may be established by the testimony of two or three witnesses.' If he refuses to listen to them, tell it to the church; and if he refuses to listen even to the church, treat him as you would a pagan or a tax collector.

Matthew 18:15-17

Life Lesson:
God wants His children to work together in His love and not be in conflict with each other. He needs us to walk together in His love so that the world will associate the church with God and His love. It is important, then, for believers to know how to resolve conflicts among themselves. The above Scripture tells us how. God tells us to go "first" to the believer who has wronged you and address the matter between the two of you. If the believer who has wronged you listens to you, then you have won him or her over. Conflict resolved. However, many of us do not like confrontation. Instead, we stew on the matter and play it over again in our mind. We are then quick to find another friend to talk to about how so-and-so hurt you, wronged you, or was not nice to you. This is not what God instructs us to do. Even though it is easier for you to go talk to someone else about the other believer, in the long run, it just causes your friend to carry a grudge against the person who wronged you and does not create a loving or productive solution. It is important for us personally to resolve our conflicts because God wants His children to be walking in love

and unity for His glory. There are times when you do confront the person who wronged you and that person will not listen. He or she is stuck in his or her position and will not budge. God tells us, as a second step, to bring one or two others along to try to resolve the matter. If that does not work, then you have done what you can to resolve the matter. Hold that person up to the Lord in prayer and forgive him or her and move on.

Confession:

I resolve in my life to address conflict first with the believer who has wronged me.

Prayer:

Heavenly Father,

Give me the grace and strength to deal with conflict, as You would have me do. In all of my interactions and relationships with others, I ask for Your love and Your wisdom to prevail. Through the power of Your Holy Spirit, I pray for unity within the body of Christ. Amen.

THIS LITTLE LIGHT OF MINE

The Word of God:

This is the message we have heard from him and declare to you: God is light; in him there is no darkness at all.

1 John 1:5

This is the verdict: Light has come into the world, but men loved darkness instead of light because their deeds were evil. Everyone who does evil hates the light, and will not come into the light for fear that his deeds will be exposed. But whoever lives by the truth comes into the light, so that it may be seen plainly that what he has done has been done through God.

John 3:19-22

Your eye is the lamp of your body. When your eyes are good, your whole body also is full of light. But when they are bad, your body also is full of darkness. See to it, then, that the light within you is not darkness. Therefore, if your whole body is full of light, and no part of it dark, it will be completely lighted, as when the light of a lamp shines on you.

Luke 11:34-36

Life Lesson:

Most of us have heard this children's song:

This little light of mine,
I'm gonna let it shine.

This little light of mine,
I'm gonna let it shine.

This little light of mine,
I'm gonna let it shine,

Let it shine,

Let it shine,

Let it shine!

God is light. When you have accepted Jesus as Lord, then you have the light of God inside of you. As God's children, we committed to let our light shine and walk in the love of Jesus. There are those who do not know the Lord and do evil against you. You may be saying to yourself right now, "It is hard to walk in the light because I am not accepted, I am not liked." It is important to understand that "evil hates the light." Peer pressure is tough; we want to fit in, and we want to be liked because it makes us feel good. But feelings should not govern our actions. God's Word should govern our lives. You are in God, God is love, and therefore, you are called to love, regardless of what those in the world do. The people who walk in darkness do not know love because they are not in God. Do not expect the world to love you. You have to choose to walk in love anyway. Set your priorities straight and focus on pleasing God in every relationship in your life. Go ahead, let your light shine; let it shine, let it shine, let it shine.

Confession:

God is light, and in Him there is no darkness at all. I choose to walk in the light and let my light shine for the world to see so that God may be glorified in my life.

Prayer:

Heavenly Father,

I thank You for Your Son, Jesus, who is the light. I thank You, Lord, that Your life fills me and I shine for You. Help me, Lord, to never let my light be hidden. Let it shine, let it shine, let it shine. Amen.

NO FEAR HERE!

The Word of God:

Have I not commanded you? Be strong and of good courage; do not be afraid, nor be dismayed, for the Lord your God is with you wherever you go.

Joshua 1:9 NKJV

For God has not given us a spirit of fear, but of power and of love and of a sound mind.

2 Timothy 1:7 NKJV

For you did not receive the spirit of bondage again to fear, but you received the Spirit of adoption by whom we cry out, "Abba, Father."

Romans 8:15 NKJV

Life Lesson:

The Lord has not given us a spirit of fear. This is important. You have to understand that the spirit of fear is not from God. The spirit of fear is from Satan. The spirit of fear is a spirit of bondage. There is God, and God is good. There is Satan, and he is evil. These two forces are opposites. God is love. Satan is hate. *God is faith. Satan is fear.* God is life. Satan is death. When you walk in hate, your heart is powered by Satan. When you walk around in fear, doubt, and uncertainty, your heartstrings are connected with the forces of Satan. The Lord did not *ask* you, He "commanded" you to be strong and of good courage and not to be afraid or dismayed. We are to have faith that God is with us wherever we go. We have to retrain our way of thinking in order to walk in faith and not fear. The forces of this world automatically flow in fear. We are told that if we want to be a good parent, we are supposed to worry over our children. This is not so and is not of the Lord. God would have you make positive Word confessions in faith over your life and the lives of your children. When doubt starts to enter in, stop it immediately and say out loud, "For God has not given me a spirit of fear, but of power and of love and of a sound mind. I do not receive a spirit of fear." This takes time, and you have to purpose in your heart that you will not allow yourself to operate in fear. Cut those soul ties with fear today. Cut off the power of Satan to control your life. Rise up and obey God's commandment. Be strong and of good courage. No fear here!

Confession:

For the Lord has not given me a spirit of fear, but of power, of love, and of a sound mind. No fear here.

Prayer:

Heavenly Father,

Thank You for the spirit of faith, of power, of love, and of a sound mind. Keep me, Father; keep me in Your tender care all of the days of my life. No fear here, Lord. Amen.

YOU NEVER RISE ABOVE YOUR CONFESSION

The Word of God:

Be imitators of God, therefore, as dearly loved children and live a life of love, just as Christ loved us and gave himself up for us as a fragrant offering and sacrifice to God.

Ephesians 5:1-2

When He had called the multitude to Himself, He said to them, "Hear and understand: Not what goes into the mouth defiles a man; but what comes out of the mouth, this defiles a man."

Matthew 15:10-11 NKJV

That if you confess with your mouth, "Jesus is Lord," and believe in your heart that God raised him from the dead, you will be saved. For it is with your heart that you believe and are justified, and it is with your mouth that you confess and are saved.

Romans 10:9-10

Do not conform any longer to the pattern of this world, but be transformed by the renewing of your mind. Then you will be able to test and approve what God's will is—his good, pleasing and perfect will.

Romans 12:2

Life Lesson:

If you want to be an imitator of God, you need to start talking like Him. How does He talk? Look to His Word. You may say, "Why is it so important that I speak the promises of God?" The answer is, "Your life depends upon it." You used your mouth to become His child and find eternal life in heaven. You confessed with your mouth that Jesus is Lord and believed in your heart that God raised Him from the dead. It is easy to determine what is in your heart by the words that come out of your mouth. What you think is what you believe, and what you believe, you confess. Let me say that again. What you think is what you believe, and what you believe is what you confess. Wrong thinking produces wrong believing. Wrong believing produces wrong confessions. Wrong confessions produce wrong actions. It is what comes out of your mouth that defiles you. Defiles means to make filthy, pollute, or corrupt. That's right, if your mouth is talking against the promises of God like curses, bitterness, fear, doubt, anger, rage, sickness, jealousy, pride, hate, and all other evil speaking, then you are corrupting yourself. Get in the Word of God, and start aligning your thinking, believing, and speaking with God. Be transformed with the renewing of your mind with God's Word. Your life depends upon it.

Confession:

I no longer conform to the pattern of this world, but I am transformed by the renewing of my mind. I choose to renew my mind daily with the Word of God.

Prayer:

Heavenly Father,

So many times, Lord, I have chosen words of corruption instead of Your Word of life. I ask You to forgive me, Lord. Amen.

TIME TO TRUST

The Word of God:

I have hidden your word in my heart that I might not sin against you.

Psalm 119:11

I will say of the Lord, He is my refuge and my fortress, My God, in whom I trust.

Psalm 91:2

Trust in the Lord with all your heart and lean not on your own understanding; in all your ways acknowledge him, and he will make your paths straight.

Proverbs 3:5

We live by faith, not by sight.

2 Corinthians 5:7

"For my thoughts are not your thoughts, neither are your ways my ways," declares the Lord. "As the heavens are higher than the earth, so are my ways higher than your ways and my thoughts than your thoughts."

Isaiah 55:8-9

Life Lesson:

One of the most difficult things for a person to do is release control of his or her life and trust. The Lord commands us to trust in Him with all of our heart and not lean on our own understanding. How do we not lean on our own understanding? We have to understand that our thoughts and ways are not the thoughts and ways of the Lord. His are higher. To better understand His thoughts and ways, we read the Word of God and meditate on it. To meditate does not mean to zone into "nothingness" with repetition. To meditate is to take a Scripture and think deeply and continuously about it. To reflect and ponder God's Word so that your spirit and mind come together. This uniting of your spirit and mind builds your capacity to release your faith. We seek His knowledge, wisdom, and understanding through His Word. We take His Word and hide it in our hearts. The Word of God is alive. We serve a living God. He is our refuge and our fortress. When times of trouble come upon us, we have a reservoir of His Word that we can draw upon. We do not keep our eyes fixed upon the darkness of our circumstances. Nor do we walk around with a dark cloud surrounding us and complain. No, we are children of the King. We draw close to our God, we pray the promise, and then praise Him for the answers. Our praises usher in the presence of the Lord. His Word strengthens our faith. It is God in whom we trust.

Confession:

I trust in the Lord with all of my heart and lean not on my own understanding. In all of my ways I acknowledge God, and He makes my paths straight.

Prayer:

Heavenly Father,

I thank You, Lord, for being my Refuge and my Fortress, my God, in whom I can trust. Bring to my remembrance a Word in season for each and every challenge and difficulty that I face in my life. Fill me with Your knowledge, wisdom, and understanding. Amen.

I FORGOT

The Word of God:

I, even I, am He that blotteth out thy transgressions for mine own sake, and will not remember thy sins.

Isaiah 43:25 KJV

If we confess our sins, he is faithful and just and will forgive us our sins and purify us from all unrighteousness.

1 John 1:9

Love is patient, love is kind. It does not envy, it does not boast, it is not proud. It is not rude, it is not self-seeking, it is not easily angered, it keeps no record of wrongs.

1 Corinthians 13:4-5

God made him who had no sin to be sin for us, so that in him we might become the righteousness of God.

2 Corinthians 5:21

Life Lesson:

Even though we have confessed our sins to God, so many of us walk around with "sin consciousness." We keep a record of all of our wrongs. We also keep a record of other people's wrongs to make us feel better. This is "sin consciousness." God does not want us to walk around thinking we are "a poor old sinner." Jesus gave His life so we can be "free from sin" and walk in His "righteousness." The way we can live free from sin is to confess our sin to God and ask for forgiveness. We repent and determine to change the way we live. God is our Father. Just like our parents think love thoughts about their children, God thinks love thoughts about you. God does not want to keep a record of your wrongs. He is love, and

He loves you with a perfect and everlasting love. The Spirit of God inside of you will impress upon you that you have done something wrong. When this happens, confess your sin to God and earnestly turn away from that wrong. When you make a choice to turn toward God, He not only forgives and forgets that sin, but He also purifies you from all unrighteousness. So if you have been purified from all unrighteousness, you have right standing with God. We are to remain in Jesus so we can walk in His love. "Love . . . keeps no record of wrongs." Be in tune with your spirit and earnestly confess your sins and turn away from that sin. Keep focused on Jesus and throw away that record of wrongs.

Confession/Prayer:
Heavenly Father,

Forgive me, for I have sinned against You and others in thought, word, and deed. I have been quick to anger and have not chosen to walk in patience and kindness. I have kept a record of wrongs. I have been a grudge holder and have judged others when I should not. I ask, in the name of Jesus, that You put into my heart Your heart, the heart that beats with the very heartbeat of heaven. Amen.

GRACE:
FREELY GIVEN, UNMERITED FAVOR AND LOVE OF GOD

The Word of God:

For since the creation of the world God's invisible qualities—his eternal power and divine nature—have been clearly seen, being understood from what has been made, so that men are without excuse.

Romans 1:20

This righteousness from God comes through faith in Jesus Christ to all who believe. There is no difference, for all have sinned and fall short of the glory of God, and are justified freely by his grace through the redemption that came by Christ Jesus.

Romans 3:22-24

For the grace of God that brings salvation has appeared to all men.

Titus 2:11

But because of his great love for us, God, who is rich in mercy, made us alive with Christ even when we were dead in transgressions—it is by grace you have been saved. And God raised us up with Christ and seated us with him in the heavenly realms in Christ Jesus, in order that in the coming ages he might show the incomparable riches of his grace, expressed in his kindness to us in Christ Jesus. For it is by grace you have been saved, through faith—and this not from yourselves, it is the gift of God—not by works, so that no one can boast. For we are God's workmanship, created in Christ Jesus to do good works, which God prepared in advance for us to do.

Ephesians 2:4-10

Life Lesson:

We as believers are to follow and obey the Great Commission from Jesus, "Therefore, go and make disciples of all nations, baptizing them in the name of the Father and of the Son and of the Holy Spirit, and teaching them to obey everything I have commanded you" (Matthew 28:19). I have heard people say, "I am concerned about those people who have grown up with another religion, or what about people who are in remote locations?" The answer is God's grace. The Word of God tells us, "The grace of God that brings salvation has appeared to all men" (Titus 2:11). Not just a few men, but all men. God uses His Spirit, His people, and whatever He needs to reveal His grace. Salvation is a gift of grace from God through His Son, Jesus, who died for our sins and was resurrected from the dead. This gift of salvation is extended by grace and received by us through faith in Jesus Christ as our Lord and Savior. We were once slaves to sin under the dominion of the devil, and now we are free from the law, credited with the righteousness of Jesus, and under the dominion of God. This gift of salvation is not by our works, but through God's grace. Receive today. Amazing grace!

Confession:

It is by grace that I have been saved through faith, and this is not from me; it is the gift of God.

Prayer:

Heavenly Father,

Amazing grace that offers the free gift of salvation to all men. Let earth receive her King. Amen.

GOD IS WAITING

The Word of God:

Without faith it is impossible to please God, because anyone who comes to Him must believe that He exists and that He rewards those who earnestly seek Him.

Hebrews 11:6

Now faith is being sure of what we hope for and certain of what we do not see.

Hebrews 11:1

Love never fails.

1 Corinthians 13:8

Life Lesson:

There it is in black and white. You must believe that God exists, that He rewards those who earnestly seek Him. Without faith it is impossible to please God. Do you want to please God? "I do." The first step to pleasing God is to believe that God exists. The second step to pleasing God is to earnestly seek Him. To earnestly seek Him means to hunger for God, to long for Him, to pursue Him with all of your heart. If you want to get to know someone, then you spend time with him or her. You want to hear and listen to what the person says. You want to be with that person and share with him or her. This is the desire of the Lord's heart, that we earnestly seek Him by reading His Word, praying to Him, spending time listening to Him. We are to seek Him for solutions to our problems. He wants us to cast all of our cares upon Him. *He desires that we walk out our lives the way He would have us walk.* And we must have faith. Without faith it is impossible to please God. "Faith in what?" you might ask. Faith that there is a God.

Faith in His promises. Faith that He can perform those promises in your life. Faith that Jesus is the Son of God. Faith that He loves you. Faith that love never fails. Start today; seek God, praise God, worship God, and surrender to Him. God wants to reward you. God wants to bless you. He is waiting to pour out His love and grace upon you.

Confession:

God, I believe that You exist and that You reward those who earnestly seek You.

Prayer:

Heavenly Father,

It is the desire of my heart to please You. May I reflect Your love in everything I do. Help me, Lord, to earnestly seek You. Amen.

LIFE FRUIT

The Word of God:

But seek first the kingdom of God and His righteousness, and all these things shall be added to you.

Matthew 6:33 NKJV

But if you are led by the Spirit, you are not under law. The acts of the sinful nature are obvious: sexual immorality, impurity and debauchery; idolatry and witchcraft; hatred, discord, jealousy, fits of rage, selfish ambition, dissensions, factions and envy; drunkenness, orgies, and the like. I warn you, as I did before, that those who live like this will not inherit the kingdom of God. But the fruit of the Spirit is love, joy, peace, patience, kindness, goodness, faithfulness, gentleness and self-control. Against such things there is no law. Those who belong to Christ Jesus have crucified the sinful nature with its passions and desires. Since we live by the Spirit, let us keep in step with the Spirit.

Galatians 5:18-25

Life Lesson:

We have all sorts of ways of measuring productivity and success in our lives. We look at report cards to determine how well our children are doing, companies measure the number of units sold to determine success in the workplace, and we count the number of push-ups, sit-ups, and minutes per mile to determine physical fitness. All of these are the world's measurements of success. We pattern our lives around these sorts of measurements. We allow these measurements to determine success in life, and we judge others by these measurements. If you are born again, top priority in your life should be structuring your life around what God tells us is success. God tells us to "seek first the kingdom of God and His righteousness." Those who seek God and make God first in their lives are a success. One indicator to determine whether you are seeking first the kingdom of God in your life is to look at your "fruit." What "fruit" are you bringing forth in your life? The Lord tells us that if we are living out our lives with acts of our sinful nature, then we will not inherit the kingdom of God. Are your relationships with others revealing the love of Jesus, or are you always in strife? Are you focused on those around you in need, or are you striving for your own ambitions? Are you walking in gentleness and self-control, or are you prone to fits of rage and anger? Are you joyful because the Lord meets all of your needs according to His riches in glory in Christ Jesus, or are you down because everyone else has more than you do (walking in jealousy and envy)? Are you seeking first the kingdom of God?

Confession:

I live by the Spirit and keep in step with the Spirit of God. I seek first the kingdom of God and His righteousness.

Prayer:

Heavenly Father,

I desire to walk out my every day in Your Holy Spirit, always keeping in step with You, Lord. I pray that my life bear an abundance of Your fruit, Lord. Help me to walk in love, joy, peace, patience, kindness, goodness, gentleness, and self-control. In Jesus' name I pray. Amen.

YOU, YOU, YOU—HE LOVES YOU!

The Word of God:

Indeed, the very hairs of your head are all numbered. Don't be afraid; you are worth more than many sparrows.

Luke 12:7

See, I have engraved you on the palms of my hands; your walls are forever before me.

Isaiah 49:16

Therefore I tell you, do not worry about your life, what you will eat or drink; or about your body, what you will wear. Is not life more important than food, and the body more important than clothes? Look at the birds of the air; they do not sow or reap or store away in barns, and yet your heavenly Father feeds them. Are you not much more valuable than they? Who of you by worrying can add a single hour to his life?

Matthew 6:25-27

I in them and you in me. May they be brought to complete unity to let the world know that you sent me and have loved them even as you have loved me.

John 17:23

Life Lesson:

God loves you. You might say, "Yes, I know He loves me, but He does not care about every detail of my life. I do not need to bother God with the small matters in my life; He is too busy with world issues." Oh, really? If God does not care about every detail of your life, then why does He know the number of every hair on your head? Why does He have you engraved

127

on the palms of His hands? God is making sure that the birds of the air are fed; don't you think that you are more valuable to God than the birds? We have a God who cares about every detail of your life and loves you beyond your comprehension. How much does God love you? God loves you just as much as He loves Jesus. I cannot imagine any more love than God has for His Son, who was perfect. Think about that, God loves you just as much as He loves Jesus. You might be saying right now, "You do not know my past. You do not know my sins. I am just too sinful for God." God demonstrated His love for us, that even while we were sinners, Christ died for us (Romans 5:8). We think that our sin makes us worthless to God. You are His child, and you are priceless. God already knows your sins. He wants you to come to Him and repent of your sins so you can receive forgiveness and He can heal you. God is love. Embrace the love of the Father in your life, and give Him all of your love. Make that love connection today.

Confession:
God loves me just as much as He loves Jesus!

Prayer:
Heavenly Father,

I open my heart wide to receive Your love and all that You have for me. I love You, Lord, from the bottom of my heart. Amen.

THE WINNER'S WALK!

The Word of God:

God is not a man, that he should lie, not a son of man, that he should change his mind. Does he speak and then not act? Does he promise and not fulfill?

Numbers 23:19

. . . so is my word that goes out from my mouth: It will not return to me empty, but will accomplish what I desire and achieve the purpose for which I sent it.

Isaiah 55:11

. . . being fully persuaded that God had power to do what He had promised.

Romans 4:21

What is impossible with men is possible with God.

Luke 18:27

Let the word of Christ dwell in you richly as you teach and admonish one another with all wisdom, and as you sing psalms, hymns and spiritual songs with gratitude in your hearts to God.

Colossians 3:16

Life Lesson:

So you have just read a book regarding the Word of God. You might say to yourself, "This is fine reading, but this does not help me understand the Bible." The only way to understand the Bible is through the Holy Spirit. God is a Spirit. The Word of God becomes alive for you through the Holy Spirit. When you accepted Jesus into your heart, God's

Holy Spirit came inside of you. As you sit down to read and meditate on the Word of God, ask the Holy Spirit to help you, to enlighten you, to highlight a Scripture for you, to lead you, and to help you understand. The Holy Spirit of God is your Helper and your Counselor. He will teach you all things. God is able to help you, through the power of His Holy Spirit, to understand His Word. Nothing is impossible with God. He wants you to stand in faith on His promises in His Word, and He wants you to know that His Word is His truth. So start reading and studying. Underline and take notes in your Bible. Start your readings with the book of John and then move to the other Gospels in the New Testament (Matthew, Mark, and Luke). As you read through the New Testament, notice the phrases "in Him" or "in Christ." These are key phrases to help you better understand who you are in Christ Jesus. You can read different translations of the Bible, such as the Amplified Bible. You can work with various study helps, such as a biblical dictionary or a concordance, such as Strong's Exhaustive Concordance. Put the Word first in your life and walk the winner's walk.

Confession:

Nothing is impossible with God. God's Word always accomplishes what God desires and achieves the purposes for which God sent it.

Prayer:

Heavenly Father,

Help me to understand Your Word as I should, Lord. Enlighten me every step of the way. Thank You, Lord. Amen.

GIVE IT UP FOR THE LORD!

The Word of God:

Submit yourselves, then, to God. Resist the devil, and he will flee from you. Come near to God and he will come near to you. Wash your hands, you sinners, and purify your hearts, you double-minded. Humble yourselves before the Lord, and he will lift you up.

James 4:7-8, 10

. . . and every tongue confess that Jesus Christ is Lord, to the glory of God the Father.

Philippians 2:11

And whatever you do, whether in word or deed, do it all in the name of the Lord Jesus, giving thanks to God the Father through him.

Colossians 3:17

In the year that King Uzziah died, I saw the Lord seated on a throne, high and exalted, and the train of his robe filled the temple. Above him were seraphs, each with six wings: With two wings they covered their faces, with two they covered their feet, and with two they were flying. And they were calling to one another: "Holy, holy, holy is the Lord Almighty; the whole earth is full of his glory."

Isaiah 6:1-3

Life Lesson:

"Holy, holy, holy is the Lord Almighty; the whole earth is full of His glory." We were made to worship the Lord. We were made to give the Lord our hearts and love Him with everything we have. Give it up for the Lord and worship Him.

131

"Draw near to God, and He will draw near to you." "Submit to the Lord." Humble yourself before Him. Purify and cleanse your hearts from any sin in your life (confess and turn away from your sin and turn to God). Put aside the things in your life that create distractions, such as television, cell phones, Internet, and video games. Start today and spend one-on-one time daily with the Lord. Give Him your undivided attention. Turn on some praise-and-worship music and minister to the Lord. Come to His gates with thanksgiving, acknowledging all that He has done for you. Enter His courts with praise, acknowledging who He is. Lift your voice and make a joyful noise to the Lord. Tell the Lord out loud that you love Him with all of your heart, and mean it. Take time and really get to know God, and He will lift you up.

Confession:

"Holy, holy, holy is the Lord Almighty; the whole earth is full of His glory."

Prayer:

Heavenly Father,

I fix my gaze upon You, Lord, for You are holy. Your Word says that You are seated on a throne, high and exalted, and the train of Your robe fills the temple. You truly are Lord. Holy, holy, holy are You, Lord Almighty. The whole earth is full of Your glory. Amen.

<u>PRAYER OF SALVATION</u>

Heavenly Father,

Your Word says in Acts 2:21, "And everyone who calls on the name of the Lord will be saved." I come to You today and call upon the name of Jesus. I ask You to come into my heart, Lord Jesus. Come in today, come in to stay, come into my heart, Lord Jesus.

Your Word tells me in Romans 10:9, " That if you confess with your mouth, 'Jesus is Lord,' and believe in your heart that God raised him from the dead, you will be saved."

I believe it in my heart, and I confess it with my mouth that Jesus is Lord and that Jesus has been raised from the dead.

I believe right here and now that I am saved. I confess that I am reborn. I am a Christian. I am a child of God Almighty. Thank You, Lord. I give You all of the praise and the honor and the glory.
Amen.

PRAYING FOR THE SALVATION OF A LOVED ONE

Heavenly Father,

I come to You today believing Your Word, which tells us that You desire that all men should be saved, so I lift up to You today _____. I plead the blood of Jesus over _____. In the name of Jesus, I break the power of Satan and all assignments and activities of Satan in the life of _____. I pray, Lord, that You would send the perfect laborers to deliver the message of the gospel in such a way that _____ will listen, understand, and receive Jesus as the Lord over _____'s life.

Fill _____ with the knowledge, wisdom, and understanding of You, Lord. Pour out Your Holy Spirit upon _____. I know that Your Word does not return to You void. I am believing right now and thanking you right now for the salvation of _____. I know that You, Lord, watch over Your Word to perform it. Thank You, Lord.

My confession of faith is that "God has begun a good work in _____'s life, and God will perform it and bring it to completion."

In the name of Jesus I pray.
Amen.

Scripture References: 2 Peter 3:9, Matthew 18:18, Matthew 9:37-38, James 1:5, Isaiah 55:11, Jeremiah 1:12, and Philippians 1:6.

He replied, 'Blessed rather are those who hear the word of God and obey it'.

Luke 11:28

ABOUT THE AUTHOR

This is the first book written by Deborah Harwood. The "Life Lessons" are topics and questions that have been asked in real life by various friends and family members. As a business lawyer for over 25 years, Deborah Harwood understands the importance of words and His Word. It is her desire that this book bless the Lord and those who read it. She resides in the Pacific Northwest with her husband and two teenage children.

ABOUT THE ARTIST

Sally Bertine Greve has a lifelong love of the creative arts. In recent years, she has discovered a love for the fluid, spontaneous properties of transparent watercolors. She seeks to dedicate her artwork to the glory of God. She is the mother of three children and grandmother of four grandchildren. She resides in the Midwest.

Printed in USA

ISBN 978-0-615-26565-0